THATCHER'S BRITAIN

Also by Terry Coleman

Novels
A Girl for the Afternoons
Southern Cross
Thanksgiving

History
The Railway Navvies
Passage to America
The Liners

Collected Journalism
The Only True History
The Scented Brawl
Movers & Shakers

Others
Providence & Mr Hardy
(with Lois Deacon)

An Indiscretion in the Life of an Heiress
(editor)

Thatcher's Britain

A Journey through the
Promised Lands

TERRY COLEMAN

BANTAM PRESS

LONDON · NEW YORK · TORONTO · SYDNEY · AUCKLAND

TRANSWORLD PUBLISHERS LTD
61–63 Uxbridge Road, London W5 5SA

TRANSWORLD PUBLISHERS (AUSTRALIA) PTY LTD
15–23 Helles Avenue, Moorebank, NSW 2170

TRANSWORLD PUBLISHERS (NZ) LTD
Cnr Moselle and Waipareira Aves,
Henderson, Auckland

Published 1987 by Bantam Press,
a division of Transworld Publishers Ltd
Copyright © Terry Coleman 1987

British Library Cataloguing in Publication Data
Coleman, Terry
Thatcher's Britain: a journey
through the promised lands.
1. Great Britain. *Parliament –*
Elections, 1987 2. Voting – Great Britain
I. Title
324.941′0858′0924   JN956

ISBN 0-593-01493-6

Photoset by Rowland Phototypesetting Ltd
Bury St Edmunds, Suffolk
Printed in Great Britain by
Biddles Ltd, Guildford and King's Lynn

Contents

FOR TOM

A Woman Of The Greatest Spirit

Acknowledgments

I have been writing about politics and politicians, on and off, for twenty-three years, mostly for the *Guardian* but also, briefly, for the *Daily Mail*. I covered the last election for the *Guardian*. I express my thanks for that opportunity to Peter Preston, the Editor, and to Richard Gott, Features Editor. I should perhaps say, in their defence, that the ways I see things in this book are not necessarily the way the *Guardian* sees them. There is no harm in that, either way.

Foreword

I covered the election of 1987 as a reporter, sometimes travelling with the party leaders, sometimes going where they did not go. This book does not claim to be a history of the campaign, much less a political analysis: this was the seventh general election I have covered, and by now I know better than to think my analysis would be better than any other man's analysis. So this is an idiosyncratic picture – made up of many fragments – of the parties, the politicians, the people whose votes they sought, and of the country as it revealed itself during the course of the campaign. It is what I saw and heard, and thought I understood – or knew I did not understand. It is one man's view of Thatcher's Britain.

THATCHER'S BRITAIN

ONE

The Frisk, and a Tale of Two Certainties

The general election of 1987 began for me with a clear view of two certainties. The first certainty was that demonstrated by Mrs Thatcher as she began her election campaign at a rapturous rally in Perth, confident that Britain had been revived and restored by her and now bore what she called a proud presence in the world. The second certainty was that shown by people in a derelict city in the north of England, who were confident, for their part, that if Jesus were to make his second coming there and then, Mrs Thatcher would nail him to a cross. They believed it.

The day of the Perth rally was a Friday. There were four weeks, all but a day, to go until the poll. The newspapers were reporting a coup in Fiji. Lieutenant-Colonel Rubuka – ex-Sandhurst, and formerly an international rugby player for Fiji – had strolled into Parliament, announced that this was a takeover, and marched the MPs to barracks where he courteously wined and dined them while HM Governor General called a state of emergency. There was a Calman cartoon in *The Times* saying, well, at least this saved the bore of having an election. At a Labour meeting in Llandudno that day, Denis Healey had called Mrs Thatcher the Catherine the Great of Finchley. He was to be a great help to her throughout the campaign, already having announced earlier that week, after a visit to Russia, that the Russians were praying for a Labour victory. The taxi driver who took me in a clapped-out Datsun from the Queen's Hotel in Perth to the city hall had a more moderate view of Mrs Thatcher – just. 'She's a brilliant leader,' he said, 'but she's nae compassion.' Furthermore, he said, as we got near the hall, he didn't think it right that the ratepayers should pay for all this. 'All this' was a regiment of policemen lining the street, more than he had ever seen in Perth before. In Perth, as everywhere else during the campaign, the threats of the IRA were taken very seriously. I told him I had seen the ruins of the Metropole Hotel at Brighton in the early morning, while they were still dragging Norman Tebbit out of the rubble, when the IRA had done their damndest to kill the whole Cabinet by blowing up the conference hotel, two years before. He said he would have no truck with the likes of them. He was glad eight of them had been ambushed and shot by British soldiers a week before in Ireland. But still, all these policemen on the rates, and so much unemployment about: it wasn't good enough.

Inside the hall, the Employment Minister, Kenneth Clarke, talked about 'you Scottish', which didn't go down too well, as you could sense, though there was still polite applause. 'We have', he said, 'rejected the world of Jack Dash, Red Robbo and Arthur Scargill.' I asked about: nobody I asked could remember Red Robbo as the union convenor who had done his best to wreck British Leyland. It was ancient history, and English ancient history at that. Then Lord Glenarthur – fourth baron, formerly of the Royal Hussars and of Aberdeen and Texas Corporate Finance Ltd., now Minister of State at the Scottish Office, and a Scot through and through – called Thatcherism a magical word and then, in a brief excursion into the history of the health service, mentioned Aneurin Bevan, whose first name he pronounced as A-new-rin. I have never heard it pronounced that way before. Could it be that Lord Glenarthur, who was only a boy at Eton when Bevan died in 1960, had never heard the name spoken before by anyone who knew the man?

The conference continued in classical Conservative fashion – that is, with no speakers even appearing to oppose the motions, which were then carried unanimously. It makes for solidarity. George Younger, formerly a Scottish Secretary – and in Scotland that office makes a man practically viceroy – then told everyone that the coming election was the most crucial since 1945. The electorate would have the chance to see off, once and for all, the Labour policy of one-sided disarmament. He said that, over its lifetime, Trident would cost each person sixteen pence a week, less than the cost of a first-class stamp. If Labour's policy were put into effect, Russia would gain in one day more than she had gained in all the years since the revolution of 1917. Then he said he must speak directly to the many thousands of men who had served in the forces, in wartime or doing their national service afterwards, and who had previously voted Labour. He could understand their having done so. But no one could now vote for Mr Kinnock's utterly irresponsible plans. For these men now to vote Conservative, for the first time in their lives, would be honourable, since by doing so they might convince the Labour Party that if it was going to have a future it must also have a proper defence policy. He had no doubt that our Prime Minister was the most outstanding leader in the West today.

At this there were cheers. But Mrs Thatcher was not due to appear until the evening rally after the conference. By the evening there were twice as many policemen round the hall as there had been earlier. To get in to the hall at all was an adventure. The Press were used to this, security having been tight ever since that Brighton bomb, before which it had been unbelievably sloppy. But the Scottish members of the conference were not used to it, not used to the endless waiting to get in, and not used to the piquancy of danger which the murdering IRA have added to political meetings. And the security in the evening, for the rally, was much stricter than for the earlier sessions of the conference.

First, everyone was gone over by a man with a machine checking for metal, and then by a second man with a machine sniffing for plastic explosives. Then came the frisk. The friskers at Perth were all young women, because while women object to being body-searched by men, men do not object to young women. So there were these young girls in uniform passing their quick hands around, above, behind, between. When it came to my turn I asked my girl whether no one ever shied at this. Hadn't any man objected? Not one? 'How could they?' she asked in that candid Scots voice, looking me in the eye as she slid a deft hand into a trouser pocket to verify that a key was just a key. Just so.

Now the Tories, when they set about it, can make a party rally into a state occasion. It is a great political gift. The drab conference of the afternoon was transformed into something different. In the hall, the vast golden-piped organ roared out 'The Bonny Bonny Banks of Loch Lomond', and suchlike rousing stuff. On each seat was a blue slip of paper giving the first eight lines of 'Land of Hope and Glory', down to 'Make thee mightier yet'. An hour beforehand, the text of Mrs Thatcher's speech had been handed out to reporters. It was thirty-seven pages long. 'Thank you', said the opening words of this advance text, 'for your spirited welcome.'

There were still fifteen minutes to go, and the platform was filling up in reverse order of precedence – first unknown officials, then Scottish MPs, then the Scottish Office ministers, and then Lord Home, who was greeted with something like love, and with cheers. Then the licensed jester, the fund raiser. It is a Tory tradition that at such rallies some creature makes a funny speech – which I have never once known to be remotely funny – and appeals for five pound notes to be stuffed into the envelopes laid out ready, along with those eight lines of 'Hope and Glory', on every seat in the hall. It is a mark of great courage and political independence for anyone on the platform, and therefore in full public view, not to applaud the rotten jokes. At annual conferences Mr John Biffen used to remain resolutely immobile, except once when he put his face in his hands. At Perth, Lord Home kept a face of Chinese impassivity, but the faithful in the audience were much amused to be told by that evening's fundraiser that the last time he spoke in that hall had been to a conference of alcoholics, and that it was nice to see so many familiar faces. He then put on a baseball cap saying 'I Love Maggie', and the donations rolled in.

Then, at 7.03, Mrs Thatcher was piped in to the tune of Scots Porage Oats. She made a triumphal entrance right up the gangway, the length of the hall. The reception was ecstatic. 'Thank you', she said, amending the advance text, 'for your *very* spirited welcome.'

'Four years ago,' she said, 'we launched a general election campaign from this very hall. You gave us a great send-off. And when the election came, it wasn't a bad result! [Laughter.] Let me just say that the people won.'

From that very hall. Well, so it had been, and I wondered if she had fixed the date of the election, as she had it in her power to do, so that this campaign too should begin at Perth. Certainly the 1983 election began there, with much the same speech. And in 1979, though she had already won by the time of the Perth conference that year, she made the first big speech of her administration there, saying, 'Well, we won, didn't we?' Could it be that so rational a woman is in fact superstitious? That would be human.

Be that as it may, she then read a run-of-the-mill speech, forty-five minutes of it. But however trite most of it was, she dominated the hall. It is an ability she shares with Ronald Reagan, though she has more of it. She is a personification of the force of Will, and there is no getting away from it. She had a few good lines too. For most of the twentieth century, it had seemed socialism was advancing and conservatism in retreat. It had seemed that the entrepreneur would disappear, along with anyone who did not either work for or depend on the Leviathan state. But how out-dated that depressing vision now seemed. It had the smell of the late 1940s about it – the atmosphere of shortages, rationing, the black market and endless restrictions. And when she said that, what she said had the smell of truth.

I must say something about the form of her speeches. First, she reads them. And they are set out for her in a peculiar way. They are typed all in capital letters. At intervals, little headlines occur, like BEWARE THE SCARES, and STRONG FOR

FREEDOM. She does not read these out. And her speeches are
set out so as to resemble free verse. Like this:

WE USED TO HEAR REGULARLY ABOUT LABOUR'S NON–NUCLEAR
   DEFENCE POLICY,
    ABOUT HOW MR KINNOCK WAS GOING TO EXPLAIN
    IT TO THE UNITED STATES AND OUR OTHER
    NATO ALLIES.
AND GAIN THEIR ACCEPTANCE.

BUT NOW ALL IS QUIET.

And talking about the abolition of rates in Scotland, which
had been pushed through in the last hours of the old Parliament, she uttered these three lines:

   THEY SAID WE COULDN'T DO IT.
   THEY SAID WE WOULDN'T DO IT.
   WE DID IT.

Here there were irresistible echoes of Doolittle the dustman
waxing eloquent in *My Fair Lady*: 'I'm willing to tell you.
I'm wanting to tell you. I'm waiting to tell you.' She could
even get away with that.

Anyway, she went on exhorting the faithful to enjoy or
endure the election but never [hushed voice] to assume, never
to take the British people for granted. Then on to a bit about
Britain's proud presence in the world and so on, and then a
five-minute ovation which she attempted to abbreviate with
modest gestures of her hands. Then the chairman told us the
world – not Britain, but the world – expected another Conservative victory, and off the leader went in triumph, pausing
to kiss Lady Home in the hall on her way out. It was a damn
good show, and he would have been a fool, I think, who
doubted that she meant every word she said.

★　★　★

Back at my hotel for dinner, I reflected on the day. I live and work in London. Since the previous general election, four years before, I had travelled quite a bit, but much more abroad than at home, most of all in America. So I was seeing many parts of Britain with a fresh eye, seeing some things for the first time, being reminded of other things I had forgotten. The comparisons that sprang to my mind were most often with London, or with the United States.

That morning I had taken the British Airways shuttle from London to Edinburgh. The plane was a new 757, in a better state than the well-worn crates that shuttle backward and forward from New York to Boston or Washington. There was also a decent breakfast. But the girl at the airport had been maddening. I had arrived early for the 9.10. The 8.10 had been delayed, was still taking on passengers, and was not full. I just went to walk on board. No, said the British Airways girl, someone at the gate had marked my ticket 9.10, so that was the plane I had to take. She would not be persuaded. Half an hour didn't matter to me either way, but it was maddening dimness on her part, an incomprehension of what shuttles are about. Throughout the United States you can walk on to any shuttle while they're practically pulling away the gangway. And as long as you've got a ticket, you can leap at the last moment on to any other domestic flight that has room. The airline is glad of the business. Passengers habitually make ten minute changes at, say, Phoenix, between one plane and another.

Then, at Edinburgh, which is a tiny airport, at not much past ten in the morning, two of the four towels in the lavatory were hanging down, used up and unreplaced. The girl at the Avis desk was explaining to two American tourists – who must constantly be asking for automatics because they have generally never driven any other kind of car – that she had no automatics. Then the drive to Perth, on a motorway better kept than any around London, and at Perth a view of the snow-covered Cairngorms. It was mid-May.

'Just a powdering,' said the receptionist at my hotel, 'a fresh fall.'

Then lunch at the Salutation Hotel, where Bonnie Prince Charlie is supposed to have stayed and which a plaque calls the oldest in Scotland – 1699. The *table d'hôte* lunch, served in a splendid room lit by a great Adam window which retains its original glass, cost only £4.75. That evening, dinner at my own hotel was not so good. In the land of Scottish beef, the roast rib did not approach what you could confidently expect at any chain restaurant anywhere I have been in the United States. But the young waiters and waitresses could not have been more pleasant and eager to please: their likes do not exist in London.

The next morning I drove back to Edinburgh, past cricket on the playing fields of Fettes, and into a grand capital city. Avis wanted its car returned to Haymarket station, the wrong one for the big trains. Just round the corner, next to Tyrie's pub, a defunct cigarette machine in the wall still asks for two shilling pieces. At Waverly station, which was the one I wanted, the other end of Princes Street, some fashionable fool has created the 'Déjà Vu' bar, with inescapable pop music inside, seats outside in a station passageway which must always be cold and draughty, and, over the tables, Parisian-style umbrellas in a place where there can never be any sun.

But the train to York was smooth and fast. The Americans on board said it was better than anything they have, which is true. Then into York station, set on a curve, a trainshed of three extraordinary spans, the roof-ribs rising from iron Corinthian columns: this is one of the great buildings of the Victorian age. It must have cost British Rail blood not to vandalize it. Even the wooden trellis arcading survives, though it was unpainted. And there waiting were local red Metrotrains, and local blue trains called Sprinters, and both were washed and clean, something I have not recently noticed of any London commuter train. I changed at York for Sheffield. The last miles into Sheffield are a vista of scrap metal yards and dereliction. It is another country. But then, this is a feeling that often comes, one way or another, upon the traveller around Britain as he enters another region, another county, or another city.

★ ★ ★

Now Sheffield is a city I have certainly seen before. I chose to go back there during the election because it has been, since 1918, the most loyal of all cities to the Labour Party, and because it is derelict, and also because in the miners' strike I saw such bitterness there as I had never seen in England before.

It was there, in 1984, that Arthur Scargill made it clear, after twenty-two weeks of the miners' strike, that he intended to go on and on and on, and also that what he wanted was not the Government's promise to keep pits open whether they paid or not, but quite simply a socialist revolution. It could hardly be complained that he made any secret of this. Historically, there was nothing new about Mr Scargill seeking not his own members' immediate advantage but some distant Promised Land. For him it would have been a socialist Promised Land, but there was little difference between that and the religious visions of earlier generations of miners. In the great miners' strike of 1844 a curious element of religion was conspicuous. Methodist preachers held wayside meetings. It was not uncommon to hear crowds praying that men brought in as strike breakers might be injured down the mines. J. L. and Barbara Hammond, the historians, also noticed the rise of a certain mysticism – not specifically Christian – a loss of faith in normal human effort, a despair of patient enquiry, a cry for infallible revelation, and an indifference to the welfare of the State. In August 1984, while Mr Scargill was conferring with his executive at a room at the university, a couple of hundred young miners stood around waiting. The *Socialist Worker* and *Spartacus* were sold. *Militant* had a good poster showing a miner, much resembling Lord Kitchener, pointing an accusing finger and saying, 'Your class needs you.'

When Mr Scargill emerged, he was asked if the NUM would do anything to stop the recent violence, to which he replied: 'Oh yes, we're appealing desperately for the police not to inflict violence upon our members.'

But at Silverwood cars had been smashed, if not by miners then by whom? He did not answer, but went on about 2,000 miners injured and finally said he was not prepared to comment on brave men and women whose only crime was fighting for the right to work.

That evening I went to the Sheffield Trades and Labour Club, and asked if I could go in and speak to some of the members. The club was in a pretty awful district, among high-rise council flats. Just down the road from the club was an old public baths which had changed its name to that of Swimming Improvement Centre. Just opposite was the Salvation Army. Anyway, I asked the club secretary, who was very friendly, and he said he would introduce me to some members of the miners' executive.

'No,' said the man he approached.

'Tell him that yourself,' said the secretary.

I then introduced myself, saying I was a reporter from the *Guardian*.

'Nothing to say to you,' said the man.

A second man said, 'See that sign?'

I asked what sign. He pointed to the green exit sign above the door. 'You're a social enemy,' he said. 'I'd like you to leave the club.'

A social enemy? Outside a Marxist tract I had never come across the phrase. I had never heard it spoken. The man cannot have known me from Adam, and if he thought the *Guardian* was a social enemy then he must have considered the miners' only remaining friends to be the *Morning Star* or *Militant*. A moderator of the Dutch Reformed Church once told me in Cape Town that I was a pagan, but he said it civilly, over tea, and after considering the evidence. At the club I looked around. None of the twenty or so members present said a word. So I said goodnight and left.

I had never forgotten that evening, and I wanted to go

back. I had asked Mr Richard Caborn, Labour MP for Sheffield Central, to take me back to the club, he had agreed, and when I got off the train from Edinburgh via York I went to see him at his committee rooms. They were just pasting up Labour's new red rose in the window. He took me to a café nearby, and we talked.

Five of the six Sheffield seats are Labour. Mr Caborn had had a majority of 16,790, which he was to increase on June 11. He is the son of a famous and much-loved communist. He was an engineering apprentice, a shop steward, and then a convenor. In 1983 he took over from Fred Mulley, the former Defence Secretary. Mr Caborn is anti-apartheid, CND, and bearded. He sounds the type and pattern of Looney Man, but I must say straightaway that he isn't, and that what follows is too brief and selective to be a reasonable account of what was a long conversation.

Look, he said, the steel industry had packed up; then heavy industry like forging. So many of the under twenty-fives were unemployed that he doubted whether the work ethic existed any more. 'They play pop music till three in the morning,' he said. 'They don't get up till ten. There's some question whether you've got to write a whole generation off.' I believe him. It's not often that an MP of the Labour left talks about so American an idea as the work ethic.

He said the city council was celebrating its sixtieth year of Labour control. The abolished metropolitan county – which had, he knew, been called the People's Republic of South Yorkshire – had done its best, with its policy of cheap bus fares, to redistribute wealth. The recent increases forced on them cost the average family another £10 a week in fares.

As to Mrs Thatcher, she had walked the streets of Moscow, on her recent visit there, with more ease than she would those of Sheffield. He had heard a man in a club say that she would walk more safely in Moscow too.

Heard a man say so in a club? Well, was that his view too? He wasn't saying that, but when she had been in

Moscow she had been at ease, buying caviar for the bloody cat.

He didn't see Russia as any menace to peace at all, did he? He said he did not, and mentioned that Sheffield was twinned with Donietz. Well, I asked, what about Hungary in 1956, Czechoslovakia in 1968, and Poland more recently? 'Not under Gorbachev,' he said. And what, he asked, about Vietnam, El Salvador, and Nicaragua?

What about the Berlin Wall, then? Good question, he said, and then I think he was for the first time evasive, mentioning fairly free movement between east and west already, different interpretations of human rights, and his hopes that the wall might come down in time. These replies wouldn't do, and I think that so ordinarily plain-speaking a man knew they wouldn't. I just said that when I had seen the wall it made me shiver. He said he had been on the border between North and South Korea, and that a GI spat at him.

Did he, incidentally, believe that Mrs Thatcher acted in good faith? 'In good faith? Yes. But I detest the faith.' That is fair enough, and a more charitable answer than you get from some members of the Labour front bench, but Mr Caborn made no bones that though he loved the human spirit he detested that of both Mrs Thatcher and the gutter press, which he believes would pillory a new-come Jesus Christ. I was to hear more about Jesus Christ later that evening.

First Mr Caborn showed me round part of his city. Near the town hall are memorials to men of the International Brigade who died fighting Franco in Spain in the 1930s. Nearby are the Peace Gardens which are often found in cities with Labour leanings. Sheffield was in the Domesday Book as Scafeld, held by Roger de Bully. In and around it are iron ore, charcoal, millstone grit, and rivers to give fast-running water. By Chaucer's time it was well known for its cutlery. It is a city, said Mr Caborn, built in seven valleys. He showed me the ruins of the Norman castle in which Mary Queen of Scots was held prisoner after 1570. Then we came to Hyde Park, great cliffs of council flats which could more profitably be ruins, but which will have to stay up for a while yet. They were built in the 1960s with great enthusiasm and in the latest architectural fashion, when Mr Roy Hattersley, now Deputy Leader of the Labour Party, was chairman of the Sheffield housing committee; but they were built high, says Mr Caborn, by central government edict. Hyde Park is now an awful city within a city, where people are cut off, with muggers for company.

We got out of the car and looked around. Nobody wants to live there any more, if he can find anywhere else. Mr Caborn has great plans for Hyde Park. He proposes to turn it into dormitories for the World Student Games of 1991 – that is, of course, if the city could attract the games there. After the Olympics, that was the second largest sporting event in the world – 110 nations taking part, and 6,500 competitors. So the idea was to do up the flats, briefly house international students there, and then persuade Sheffield university and the polytechnics to take them for their students. That way, as I understood Mr Caborn, the council would get shot of most of Hyde Park. Those flats that then remained would be let to single people. At any rate, no more families would have to live there. It was all in the future, all plans, but he hoped the games might do more for Sheffield than the televized snooker championships at the Crucible Theatre already did, and they brought in £1,500,000 a year.

Then we drove a short distance out into the suburbs, where there were no longer tower blocks, just roads of ordinary houses, but all still owned by the council. I said, look, that phrase about a property-owning democracy – that had been coined by his political opponents. But put it more plainly. Say that people wanted to own their own houses – wasn't that true? 'We have people here', he said, 'who never had a job in their lives. How should they buy a house? We have to house them. We have to protect them.'

Then we went to his own house, built, I should think, in the 1930s, the same size as all the others, but one of the few that were privately built, not by the council. He bought it years ago for a song. It is his, not the council's or anyone else's.

In her sitting room, his wife Margaret asked me how old Mrs Thatcher was. I said sixty or sixty-one, though at Perth she hadn't looked it.

Mrs Caborn: 'No, she doesn't. Say what you like, she doesn't. More's the pity.'

Mr Caborn sat down on a sofa, with his daughter Catherine at the other end, and said really there were people, many people, in the city who lived with an underlying fear that they would never get a job. Never. If he had anything to do with it, there was going to be a massive closing of the gap, the gap between the have and the have-nots.

There was a silence. Closing the gap is one thing, but Mr Caborn is, I think, an egalitarian, and that is a difficult creed, since men are so observably not equal in their abilities. Put two men behind a hedge, and within ten minutes one or the other will, without any conscious or necessary attempt on his part to do so, have demonstrated his superiority in some way or another. That's the way it is, and those who struggle against this, swim against the current. I said nothing, but Mr Caborn caught the sense of what I was not saying. 'You're the right-wing conscience of the *Guardian*,' he said. 'They told me not to see you. I said I don't give a bugger. I'll sing the same song.'

It then somehow came out in conversation that Mrs Caborn had been born in a pub in Sheffield, a pub, she said, where there was sawdust on the floor. I said my father had been too. The pub where he was born was not in Sheffield, but in Poole. It was called the Black Horse. I remembered it well as a boy, when it was run by my widowed grandmother, a tall woman, six feet tall in my memory. She ran it until she was a great age. Memory is fallible, but I think she still ran it in her eighties. Above all, I remember the sawdust on the floor. In the 1950s, when Poole council, in its well-meaning idiocy, pulled down practically the whole of that part of the old town to the left of the High Street – to build tower blocks, and only little tower blocks at that –

it demolished all the streets around the pub, and round the school which my father left when he was twelve. My own middle name is Francis. My father gave me that name after Mr Francis, who was one of his schoolmasters, a man he often talked about. I remembered the Black Horse well. When the council had almost finished laying waste to the old town, the Black Horse was the last building left standing. It stood for a while on its own, and then it too was demolished. That at any rate is what I clearly remember, the last pub in old Poole left standing, where my father was born.

'Poole?' said Mr Caborn. Before he came into Parliament he had been offered a job there. He named the company, which my father would have known. Britain may not be one nation – as what nation ever is? – but it's a small one. My father went straight from school to an engineering apprenticeship which lasted seven years. Mr Caborn, many years later, did the same. Then their lives took different routes. My father was by his late twenties manager of the factory where he had served his time. The smell of slurry – half oil, half metal turnings – permeated my childhood. It was brought home in my father's clothes. He had no interest in politics, though he voted Labour in 1945, and remained until the end of his life an honorary member of the Amalgamated Engineering Union. Mr Caborn was more active in his union and in the Labour Party. Since he was a boy he had known Fred Mulley, the previous member for Sheffield Park, which was renamed Central after the redistribution of the early eighties. Mr Mulley rose to serve in the Wilson and Callaghan cabinets. When in 1982 the constituency selection committee grew tired of him, and wanted something different, it was to Mr Caborn that they turned. Mr Caborn remains on good terms with Fred, now Lord, Mulley, which isn't always so with a new member and his deselected predecessor. Perhaps it helps if the rejected member has had the consolation of going to the Lords.

At any rate, after this talk of sawdust on pub floors, which woke vigorous memories in both of us, Mr Caborn took me to the Trades and Social Club, where I had been on that one occasion before. Did I know, he asked me, what illustrated as well as anything else the fall in purchasing power of the members, what showed how much less well-off they really were nowadays? It was this. In 1981 beer was 44p a pint, and the club takings were £4,500 to £5,000 a week. Now, in 1987, beer was 72p a pint, and the takings were £3,500 to £4,000 a week. Either there had been a growing tendency towards temperance, or, what was more likely, a man could nowadays afford only half a pint whereas before it would have been a pint.

Mr Caborn then had to leave for another engagement, and I was introduced to Mr Ken Curran, an official with the National Union of Public Employees, and Mr George Machin, the club secretary. We sat at a table with half pints in front of us. A man heard us talking and came over. He had a deep-felt grievance, which had plainly scarred his life. He wanted to talk about it. My two companions had obviously heard it all before, but they listened to it again. They would not, in courtesy, do otherwise. The man had worked many years for a company. He had stumbled upon a fiddle which was enriching some of his superiors. He refused to take part in it. Hints were dropped in his direction that some things would be better left as they were, and that the less said the better. He then made his objections clear. After a while, a pretext was found to get rid of him, and he was made redundant. He had tried to get himself reinstated, but had failed. He had sought justice, and it had been denied him. That was the story he told.

Now I had never seen the man before, but the story was familiar. It is the kind of story men come to newspaper offices with, and a reporter sits with them in reception and listens, and nine times out of ten knows that there is nothing on earth that can be done. The man may be in the right. The man may be in the wrong. There is no telling. By that time, the sequence of events is so complicated and obscured that it is almost impossible to unravel. Besides, it is a dangerous business: the story is probably of little public interest, though it is of desperate importance to the man who is telling it, but a reporter always has to be careful of libel. Newspapers are timid about libel. Libel is messy and time-consuming, and the risk of it, in an editor's view, is best avoided. The threat of a writ, the hint of a writ, just a solicitor's letter on behalf of the company or local council or government department complained against, is quite enough to cause an editor to drop a story then and there. Well, the man who came over to us in the club had such a story. When he took out some well-thumbed papers, and showed me a letter, written by himself, I took one look at the closely handwritten sheet, with its frequent use of capital letters, and knew the nature of his case, having seen many others. He was bitter that a television reporter, having expressed interest, had done nothing, and then, after repeated requests, returned all the papers to him. They were still in the original envelope in which he had sent them, unopened.

The man left. We looked at each other, and began to talk about Mrs Thatcher and the miners' strike.

Mr Machin: 'The laws were always made to apply to us, not for the higher-ups. I've been saying it's a police state for ten years.'

Mr Curran: 'England is an occupied country. It's under Norman rule.'

What, I said: look at the Thatcher eyes and hair; consider the temperament. Her, Norman?

'She's a Quisling.'

A third man, a former county councillor, then said, 'The very word Parliament comes from Norman French.'

Now I know these are only snatches of a conversation. But Quisling? Norman rule? It was surreal. But Mr Curran, who had protested against Norman rule, turned out as the evening progressed to be no joker. He several times spoke bitterly about the Highland clearances of the eighteenth century. He said it was the same in Sheffield nowadays. The industries had died, the people were no longer of any use, and were being disposed of.

Mr Machin: 'The whole history of law has been to repress the people. Look at the Enclosure Acts. They drove people into the factories.' I was then told that if Jesus Christ was reborn that day, Mrs Thatcher wouldn't wait thirty-three years this time before nailing him to a cross.

There was a lull in the conversation, and I said I had been to the club once before, during the strike, and . . .

'I know,' said Mr Machin. 'I let you in.'

Then I recognized him. He had indeed been the friendly secretary who took me over to some of the club members. He was a man who for one year up to February 1974 had been Labour MP for Dundee East, when, in a surge of patriotic feeling after the discovery of North Sea oil, the Scots Nats took the seat from him. Then he had become club secretary at Sheffield. I remembered his own friendliness, and his insistence, when his members declined to talk to me, that they should tell me so themselves. So, I said, perhaps he could tell me why they had refused, and why they had added for good measure that I was a social enemy?

'They regarded you', said Mr Machin, 'as part of the other nation.'

The talk then turned to the police, who in that strike were emphatically seen as part of the other nation, and who had arrested twenty men outside that club. These were miners from Durham and Nottinghamshire, who had come down to demonstrate, and asked if they could use the club. There were about two hundred of them. They had a buffet lunch, and a bit of a sing-song, and then they went and sat on the grass outside. Then the police arrived, and slung them into vans. One miner had a heart attack.

Mr Curran: 'The police came at them with batons, in a semi-circle outside. I let some in at the main door and they got away at the side.'

Mr Machin: 'You came along a few days after that. So they were pretty distrustful of the press.'

Mr Curran: 'I had a union car. I was stopped five times. They had the number on the computer.'

Mr Machin: 'Anyone trying to get on to the M1 was stopped. Talk about a police state.'

Did he still think that? 'I think we're moving towards it. We're quite friendly with the police now. But there were a lot of bully boys from the Met.'

Mr Curran then described the siege at the Orgreave coke depot, a few miles down the road. He was telling me how the police had lined the roads five and six deep, but at that point in his narrative a young man came into the club in rags, evidently got up for a fancy dress ball.

Mr Curran: 'Who's your tailor?'

Young man in rags: 'I'm dressed up as a miner – after the police have finished with me.'

Mr Machin: 'I think the job attracts a fair number of wrong 'uns, the police. If I saw two or three blokes attacking a copper I'd go to his aid. But you've got to be wary of the police.'

Mr Curran: 'I wouldn't say there's any hatred.'

Mr Machin: 'Just a guarded wariness.'

Mr Curran then drove me to a miners' club at Silverwood. The road ran along the Don valley, past places like Salmon Pastures where there once really were salmon, and then steel mills, and then just dereliction and ruin. A few years before, 7,000 men worked in those steel mills, but now only 700. It is no good suggesting to anyone who used to work there that the world market for steel has diminished, and that there would no longer be a market anyway for steel at the price it could now be made in Sheffield. Those who live in Sheffield, or used to work there, see only that the industry has collapsed in Mrs Thatcher's time: therefore it is her fault, her doing.

The Silverwood Miners' Club, known to everyone as the Baggin, was the place where the first soup kitchen was set up in the strike. The women's action group who set it up still meet, three years on, every Monday evening at the Bridge Inn at Rotherham. At the club, the Saturday night I was there, there was bitter talk about miners sacked and never reinstated. When they saw me sitting there with Mr Curran, men came up and told their stories.

'This man, he had four sons sacked. One was sacked for besetting. Picketing a scab's house, that means.'

'First soup kitchen in South Yorkshire this was. Eight hundred men. Just tea and soup to start off with.'

'They can keep their twopence off income tax. That's £1.20 a month to me. That's what I paid for this.' [indicating his pint of beer.]

'I've got a brother. His kids wear plastic shoes. I slip him two or three quid for cigs. Take him out for a drink now and again. Otherwise, he couldn't afford to.'

'Arthur Scargill? At Silverwood he's still King Arthur. They haven't got rid of him. His executive has asked him to keep quiet, that's all.'

'If you look back at Sheffield in 1944, it was devastated by Hitler. But it's nothing to what she's done now.'

'Right. If Labour got back tomorrow, they couldn't do anything. They couldn't start the steelworks again, because they've pulled them down.'

Mrs Gwen Mellors was one of those who ran the soup kitchen. She is a nurse, and works in a geriatric ward. In the previous two years everything had altered. They didn't have sufficient stocks of drugs. There were no longer enough nurses. Patients in pain put off asking you for something, because they knew you were too busy, run off your feet. That was shameful, people lying in pain because they wouldn't ask. Pain was the first thing. The first thing you did, you always relieved pain.

And the police had so incensed her during the strike, she said, that she wouldn't have them in the hospital waiting room. She wouldn't have them drinking cups of tea there. She'd told that to the ward sister. Since then, the police hadn't been allowed in.

I recalled a passage from Mrs Thatcher's speech of the evening before, in which she had said that spending on the National Health Service had been eight billion pounds in 1979, but had risen this year to twenty-one billions. Now, I said to Mrs Mellors, never mind what the Prime Minister's views might be, never mind what her motives might be, never mind that she might have an interest in putting things in the best light – but just consider those figures. They wouldn't have been invented, because things like that could be checked. Didn't those figures show that there had been, by any standards, a real increase in spending on health? Mrs Mellors didn't know. She could only speak of what she saw and what she knew, and said she had already told me that.

Mr Curran, who had been sitting listening, said: 'If it wasn't for the fact that people get a drink, there'd be a lot of despondency.'

But it seemed to me, as I looked round, that, never mind the drink, there was a lot of despondency anyway. There were probably three hundred people in the club. It was crowded. The car park outside was full. The cars were not new, and compared with what you would see in any American car park they were, many of them, not much better than scrap. But there was no outright poverty to be seen. The children with plastic shoes were not there. Nobody was hungry. Soup kitchens were no longer needed. But there was an immiseration of these people. This is a word I take from that week's *New Statesman*. Now that is not much of a magazine any more, though by the time of the election it had, under a new editor, recovered some of its tone and lost some of that entire bigotry and dullness which had submerged it for the previous few years. But the word immiseration, which appeared in a leading article, struck me, as I drank my beer in that club, as exact.

'I'm lucky,' said Mrs Mellors. 'I've got a telephone, I've got a car, little luxuries. We have a holiday once a year. Skegness this year.'

Did she generally go abroad? She said the only time she'd ever been abroad was to Russia and Bulgaria, with the miners' union, in the strike. The Bulgarian unions had paid for that.

What, I asked, if Mrs Thatcher did get her third term? What if she won? What then? A young miner, a face worker, answered me: 'If she does, I really do think that Broadwater Farm is going to look like a tea party. Up north anyway.'

The certainties of Sheffield and Silverwood were as deeply held as those of Perth. I do not question the good faith of anyone I listened to or spoke with all that weekend. Mrs Thatcher on the smell of the 1940s was eloquent. So were the men and women in those two clubs.

I had incidentally been in Yugoslavia the week before the general election was called. The miners were on strike there, and their demand was for a 100 per cent rise. And it was observable in the shabbiness everywhere that the people's flag was deepest grey. When in Sheffield I asked Mr Caborn to name a country where socialism had worked, he said Sweden, which is true, but Sweden is exceptional in that it's so rich in iron and timber and other things, and so sparsely populated, that any form of government could produce prosperity. And the taxes anyway are so high as to amount to an infringement of personal liberty. So I asked Mr Caborn for another example. He said Austria, which was really no more convincing, since Britain, run down as she is, is not comparable with tiny, neutral Austria.

Certainties, certainties. There was only this glimmer. As we were saying goodnight at the club, Mrs Mellors said: 'When she first came in I thought it might do the country some good. A woman. To bring up a family. But she's never ever had to want. To be honest, say she gets elected again, and she puts my sons in employment, then I tell you what, the next time she came up I'd vote for her. But she won't. Things have really gone from bad to worse.'

TWO

Joe Average and the Rainbow

I returned from Sheffield to London by train the next morning. At Sheffield station, on the platform where the London express comes in, the waiting room and buffet were both still locked at 10 a.m. The chocolate machine on the platform was not working. The train did have a buffet car, but when I went to try and get something to eat, after we had passed Leicester, there were no sandwiches, and no butter to go with the croissants which they did have. I could have a whisky, but there was no soda and no mineral water to go with it. In the lavatory, there was no running water to go with the handbasin either.

In London, the young driver of cab 2968 offered his electoral views. 'They lose the Joe Averages like me, till they get the loonies out – and the gays, and lesbians, and all the mad ideas they come out with.'

Yes? 'There's always been gays and lesbians, but you didn't have to have it rammed down your throat. Lesbian committees? I'm a working man, me.'

So much for Labour. What about the Alliance? 'Don't like the old pals act. The SDP would get my vote if they were alone. I don't like those two flying off together. One or the other. It should be one or the other.'

So he would vote Conservative? 'Yes. Me, voting for her! But that's the way it is.'

He said he lived in Dulwich, and then went on a bit about

the neighbouring London borough of Lambeth, which is a nuclear-free zone – whatever that means – and has high rates and a well advertised consciousness of all minorities and of what it calls 'gender'. 'You get rid of Red Ted,' said the driver, 'and you get Linda Bellos. A right winning double.' Red Ted Knight was the Labour leader who had been disqualified after failing to set a legal rate: he was replaced by Ms Bellos, who is black and has proclaimed herself a lesbian.

The received wisdom is that Labour fought a polished election campaign, and there is much truth in this, but the next day, at its first national press conference, the party was at it again, alienating the Joe Averages. Each party during the campaign held a press conference in London each day. A party leader can choose the topic for each press conference: he or she may then find that the reporters' questions are not obligingly addressed to that topic, but the topic can in the first place be largely determined by the nature of the statement the leader chooses to make. Now Labour, being convinced that the national Press was hostile, had already decided that Mr Kinnock would not appear at most of his party's press conferences in London. He would address the less demanding provincial Press instead, in various cities round the kingdom, where the more experienced political commentators – having in the course of their duties to hear what Mrs Thatcher chose to say each morning in London, and besides preferring the comforts of the capital to the slog of the travelling campaigns – could be relied upon not to follow him. But Mr Kinnock did choose to attend the first London conference, and the topic was that of Labour's Ministry for Women. The stars of the morning were a four-month-old baby called Amy, and a proposal for a Minister for Women, who would of course be a woman.

The place was the old familiar room in Transport House, so called because it belongs to the Transport Workers' Union, where Wilson and Callaghan held their more sober conferences. It all started with the poor child being held up for the photographers' flashlights.

'What's its name?'

'Amy.'

'This way, Amy. Come on, Amy. Look this way, Amy.'
The photography went on longer than usual because the
party was, as an official explained from the platform, having
trouble with a copier which was at that late moment still
producing the handouts. The man said that in the press
office, which he explained was in the old kitchen or the old
table tennis room, there were other leaflets we might like to
be having a look at.

One leaflet, very glossy, displayed at the top twelve
head and shoulder portraits of women, young and old,
reproduced in black and white: all these pictures showed
women in states of extreme anxiety, or pain, or at least
discontent. Then, arranged below these portraits, were
another twelve portraits of the same women, but this time
in full colour and in carefree states of excellent good health
and humour. They were, as the headline said, 'Looking
Forward to a Brighter Future for Women'. Six of the
twenty-four portraits were of black women, twenty-five
per cent as against the actual national percentage of four per
cent. Another document, a booklet of sixteen pages, gave
details of the proposals. There was to be a Minister for
Women, who would be in the Cabinet. Furthermore, since
the experience of the Australian Office of Women's Affairs
was persuasive, her department would be within the Cabinet
Office itself, to give her 'crucial access to the Prime Minister,
a position close to the centre of power in Whitehall, and the
opportunity for exerting widespread political influence'.

Up spoke Ms Jo Richardson, Labour front bench spokes-
person on women's rights and formerly chair of the party's
Black and Asian advisory group. She asserted that, under
Mrs Thatcher, women's rights had been systematically dis-
mantled, and that increasingly under the Tories women had
been forced to take jobs with low pay. Both the run-down
state of the inner cities and the isolation of the countryside
meant that many women were now afraid to leave home at
night. There would be no women's ministry under the

Conservatives. Only the privileged few would be encouraged to fly high with Mrs Thatcher.

Then Mr Kinnock rose. 'Sisters and Brothers of the Press,' he began. It was a form of address I never heard him use once again during the campaign. The gist of his diffuseness was that a Ministry for Women was necessary 'so that the deeds of delivery should follow the thoughts of action'. He was against drudgery and disadvantage, but then who is not?

The Sisters and Brothers of the Press were a bit flippant in their questions. Fine, but would there be any more women in a Labour cabinet than there had been previously? Since women constituted a majority, he said, one should maximize the number of women in government.

Ah. Would the new ministry be the size of, say, the Ministry of Agriculture? Mr Kinnock thought not. There would be a woman secretary of state, a minister of state, and one parliamentary under secretary. He took it for granted that the secretary of state would be a woman. Here Ms Richardson interjected that a staff of about three hundred would be needed, at an annual cost of £10 millions, and that it would be a fairly modest ministry.

Well, if the Prime Minister could be a woman, why couldn't the Secretary of State for Women be a man? 'That', replied Mr Kinnock, 'is an interesting conundrum.'

If a Ministry for Women, why not a Ministry for Blacks? Mr Kinnock, on the spot because he had taken a stand against black sections in constituency parties, thought these matters were of a different scale and nature.

Ms Richardson here remarked that they would be taking a look at the particular discrimination suffered by black women. She also said a bit later, apropos of what I cannot remember, that women didn't like salacious gossip.

Mr Kinnock was then photographed with the ten women on the platform, and then Baby Amy was brought back into the act.

'Hold it up, Neil.' He did hold Amy up, and the child faced more flashlights.

'Put it on your shoulder, Neil.' He did. The poor child was lugged about, looking apprehensive but behaving stoically in the cause. She did not cry. In the scrum for her elders' rights, she behaved impeccably. She was eventually handed back to her mother – Ms Harriet Harman, MP for Peckham.

The women's campaign then went out on tour, to visit factories, offices, hospitals, schools, nurseries, and shopping precincts – 'anywhere women can be found'. As the handout said, 'Labour Women Hit the Campaign Trail'. It was proposed that groups of women should make proselytizing visits to the Midlands, Norwich, Wales, Bristol, Yorkshire, and so on. It was promised that there would always be two leading trade unionists with each team.

What was exceptionable about all this was not that Labour should be making a point of women: after all, the party was, in its own words, out to 'highlight' the importance of women voting Labour. Labour was after their votes, which was fair enough. What was strange, and much noticed, was that Labour should have begun its campaign by choosing to promote any sectional interest at all, whatever it was. The Democratic 'rainbow coalition' fell to pieces in the 1984 American presidential campaign because each colour of the rainbow – blacks, women, gays, Greens – was more concerned with itself than with the whole. People who are fundamentally interested only in one single issue tend towards quirkiness. Even if they are not monomaniacs they often appear to be, and are easily caricatured as such. And it is a strange, and I think sad, fact that the most active of women politicians tend to lack the softer feminine virtues. H. L. Mencken, covering the 1932 Democratic convention that chose Roosevelt for its candidate, wrote about Niagaras of bilge, implacable factions all hating each other, and all sorts of grotesque female politicians with brassy voices. Women were on show again at the 1984 convention in San Francisco. I do not mean Geraldine Ferraro, who, in her speech accepting the vice-presidential nomination, spoke softly. I mean the likes of the Governor of Kentucky. She was a woman born in Baghdad, Kentucky, and formerly a beauty queen. There was no getting away from her because she took the chair for most of the convention. I will not go as far as Mencken, but the Democratic women were almost without exception shrill and aggressive. I remember asking myself if this wasn't strange, since persuasion is surely one of the political arts.

But to return to England, and to Labour. There it was: Labour had chosen to begin its campaign in London with one single colour from its rainbow, and to do this before the party had even published its general manifesto.

That came the next day.

THREE

Wife-Beating and Big Trees

Manifestos can be eloquent. To start, I shall take a few words at random from both the Conservative and Labour documents. From the Conservatives: 'We stand for the fullest opportunity for go and push in all ranks throughout the whole nation. This quality is part of the genius of the British people . . .' And: 'We will not permit any monkeying with the people's savings.' And: 'We must take care of our big trees.' From Labour: 'Our ultimate purpose at home is the establishment of the Socialist Commonwealth of Great Britain.' And, reviewing the record of previous capitalist governments: 'Never was so much injury done to so many by so few.'

These are words which say what they mean, but they are not from the manifestos of 1987 but from those of 1945. The manifestos then were short. The Conservatives' was pure Churchill. He wrote it himself. Labour's, openly asserting a wish for socialism and making no bones about it, used to be taken for the work of the prolix Laski pruned down by the laconic Attlee. This is very likely, but it is not the truth. It was in fact written by Michael Young, later Lord Young of Dartington, who was then a young barrister working for Labour's research department. It was then looked at by Ellen Wilkinson – formerly a suffragist, a woman who had held junior office in the wartime coalition, and a bit of a legend; she later became Minister of Education in the Attlee govern-

ment. The foreign policy bits were looked at by Patrick
Gordon-Walker, formerly with the BBC foreign service,
later to become Foreign Secretary. Then Herbert Morrison,
the Deputy Leader, had a look at it too, but writing wasn't
his strong point, so it was passed quickly to Mr Attlee
himself. It was on and off his desk in the same day. He
glanced at it and sent it to the printer.

Those were days of innocence. Things are more sophisti-
cated now. The contents of the 1987 manifestos – or at any
rate the main heads of party policy – were, for the duration
of the campaign, more or less well known, and then, afterwards, more or less forgotten. But the style of the manifestos
– the kind of words in which they were written and the way
in which they were printed and presented – revealed the
style of the parties themselves, and that remains longer in
the memory. And to some degree style is inseparable from
content and from policy, which it often helps shape. And
sometimes style will cruelly, or mercifully, expose policy
for what it is.

First, appearances. As I held them in my hands the manifestos reminded me of different kinds of junk mail that had
come unsolicited through my letter box over the years. The
Conservative manifesto – soberly printed, with thick glossy
covers, smaller in format than the others, and enclosed in a
plastic slipcase – looked very like another proposal from
American Express or Diners Club for some investment or
insurance scheme beyond my means. Labour's was larger
in format, about the same size as a Sunday paper colour
supplement, with a glossy cover printed in four colours.
My wife said it looked like a slimmer version of the catalogue
of Next, which is a sort of down-market Jaeger, selling
trendy clothes. The Alliance manifesto, in much the same
format, resembled the copious literature for the Greens
which used to arrive for our German *au pair*. Inside, everything was restless: constant underlining of passages, endless
black dots intended to draw the eye to just about every other
paragraph, and, in twenty-three pages, no fewer than sixteen
urgent topics displayed in their own little boxes. On the

cover the two Davids, both in sweaters, smiled out together from a badly over-exposed photograph – as if they were just back from a successful preserve-the-badger symposium.

Of the three, the Labour manifesto was technically much the best set and printed, as it was in their disastrous election year of 1983. And it was not the Conservatives, the Land of Hope and Glory party, which usurped the word Britain as part of its manifesto's title. It was the other parties that did that. *Britain Will Win*, said Labour. *Britain United*, said the Alliance. They had done the same in 1983, when Labour and the Alliance proposed, respectively, *New Hope for Britain* and *Working Together for Britain*. At both elections, the Tories made do with a less overtly patriotic title. Above all, Labour's was the most imperial-looking manifesto. Mr Kinnock dominated the glossy cover, complete with caring red rose in lapel and arm raised high in triumph. Mrs Thatcher's picture did not appear on the cover or anywhere in the seventy-seven pages of her party's manifesto.

Now for the words of the manifestos, the style of the writing. What was remarkable about the Conservatives' was that there was almost nothing remarkable. The compiler had obviously read the late Sir Ernest Gowers's *Plain Words*, and taken it all to heart. The manifesto showed throughout high competence in words quite unsullied by flair. The section called The World Stage came very near the beginning, whereas both the other parties put it pretty near last. But apart from making that different choice of emphasis, the writer of the Conservative document did nothing exceptional. Policies were allowed to speak for themselves. 'We are the only party that believes in lower taxation.' Or: 'Labour's policy would not mean a secure Britain but eventually a neutralist Britain. And eventually – for there can be no trifling with Soviet power – a frightened and fellow-travelling Britain . . . This election matters more for our safety and freedom than any election since the Second World War.'

Altogether, there was little detectable cant. Inner cities were spoken of when what was meant was decayed suburbs,

but that is now a pretty universal sloppiness. There was only
one piece of nonsense that leapt at you from the page. 'The
broadcasters owe it to the lively talent in the independent
sector to take more programmes from them.' *Owe* it to
them? Since when, in Mrs Thatcher's philosophy, did anyone owe anyone else a living?

Labour's manifesto was not written in words that Sir
Ernest Gowers could remotely have thought plain. And
since it so obviously was not written plain, the suspicion
had to lurk that plainness would have been politically inex-
pedient. Labour would increase, raise, end, abolish, under-
pin, take action on, and implement – above all implement
– all manner of things. Strategy was comprehensive. Fairness
was 'not just a fine word'. (But, alas, in the nature of things,
it generally is.) Some proposals, it was said, 'must take
lower priority in terms of timescale and public resources'.
What did that mean? Wait till the money was found?

Labour, with undoubted good will, proposed to legislate
for more convenient hours for doctors' surgeries to open,
and for an end to wife-beating and to all organized hunting
with hounds. Well, hounds can be restrained, but as for the
rest, how? Labour also – and these were words to be exam-
ined and relished – believed in a united Ireland, to be achieved
peacefully, democratically, and by consent. Just as Labour
would 'actively' seek a stable peace in the Middle East which
would protect the security of Israel and at the same time
recognize the right of Palestinians to self determination. And
the lamb shall lie down with the lion? Yes indeed. Very
nice. There should be a Nobel peace prize or two in that.
But what wool! What pious fluff!

Were such words capable of any real meaning? Any self-
respecting Chartist labourer of the 1830s, with a parish
school education, could have taken up his slate and a bit of
chalk and done better. And the only reference to socialism
I could find in the whole manifesto called it 'democratic
socialism'. One of the few bits which sounded as if it meant
what it said was in the introduction signed by Mr Kinnock,
where he said that Britain couldn't afford any more of the

Tories' 'run–down, sell–off, and split–up'. The only strength of the whole manifesto was its comparative brevity. It was half the length of the Conservatives', which at 20,000 words or so was about a quarter the length of a decent novel.

The Alliance manifesto was, on the whole, one in which the teaching of mathematics was described as the boosting of numeracy. But it had its strong points. Listen to this: 'We will curb the sale of knuckledusters, battle knives, spiked shoe straps, cross-bows, and catapults.' What about siege ladders too? There would also be a law to make British Telecom keep its telephone boxes in repair, which was a brave promise to make. Apart from that, class divisions would be abolished 'in the workplace'. (At work?) And the Alliance wanted proportional representation, devolution, more upland beef, and better kept walls, hedges, footpaths, and meadows. It wanted more infrastructure as well as more fairness. It was determined to end South Africa's occupation of Namibia, as if there were anything it could do about it. The Alliance also wanted Shared Earth, which it put in one of its little ruled-off boxes. This meant giving money to poor countries, but the very phrase Shared Earth, which was probably dreamed up by some Young Liberal and left in as part of the two-party compromise deal, had for me a strong echo of City Harvest. This is a fashionable piece of Manhattan radical chic. You give a party for two hundred friends and clients at your place in the East 60s, and next morning the volunteer from City Harvest comes and takes away all the leftover smoked salmon canapés and hands them out to the destitute down in the Bowery.

The Alliance was especially strong, stronger even than Labour, on what is known as the 'community'. Wherever this word occurred it was a challenge to the ingenuity of the reader to supply an appropriate meaning. There generally was some possible meaning. A community as encountered in those Alliance pages could mean a club, a town, a city, an island, blacks, a broken-down council estate, or the people living in a street like, say, Coronation Street. There was also a mention of 'community architecture' which, in a rather unlikely way, found itself in the same sentence as a concern for the quality of life. The Alliance also wanted to 'end the twilight ghettos', and if I used my imagination I could envisage such a place. And to the Alliance fell the distinction of having the only manifesto to mention the class struggle. This took place, naturally, in inner cities.

So altogether, whether you liked her kind of forestry or not, the only big trees in those manifestos belonged to Mrs Thatcher. The Alliance did say it would place more emphasis on broad-leaved species. And the Alliance did, in one respect, break some sort of mould. It did not call its manifesto a manifesto at all. The only party of the three to have no chance whatever of forming a government, and which never once claimed that it did, called its manifesto a Programme, a 'guidebook for government'.

What was also fascinating about the manifestos was the way in which their first presentation in public reflected the style of the documents and of the parties' leaders.

Labour's was presented not at shabby old Transport House but in the Churchill auditorium of the new and hideous conference centre at Westminster. It was splendidly stage-managed. Behind a new-style podium, with very little red about it, only Labour's red rose at one side, sat the Shadow Cabinet. The podium remained empty. Then, 'Lights', called someone. Then, 'Stand by.' Then, 'Music.' And to the strains of his bit of Brahms that had become Labour's signature tune, Mr Kinnock strode to the rostrum, with a television crew walking ritually backwards in front of him to film him as he came. It was a triumphal entry. Whoever devised it deserved an Oscar. The style was widely thought to be new.

It wasn't. Mr Kinnock had been working on it for a long time. His rehearsals went back to February 1984, when Labour was picking itself up after the demoralizing loss of the 1983 election. In the autumn of 1983 Mr Kinnock was elected leader. He settled in, and then, the following February, for no reason apparent at the time, the party issued pressing invitations to a rally at Newcastle. Those who accepted did so because they thought something new was to be said. It wasn't. Beforehand, Mr Kinnock did a three-minute pop video with Tracy Ulmann, which was shown on Tyne Tees Television. Then – in the city of the Romans, of George and Robert Stephenson, and of Grey of the Reform Bill – he appeared not in one of the vast, derelict cinemas or tatty theatres of party tradition but in a new auditorium in a new shopping centre. And what he said did not amount to much. He said the only thing Mrs Thatcher understood was, 'Yes, Prime Minister, three bags full.' He said that he wanted to set the people free, though he did not say how. He said that people longed for serenity. He said it was no good his listeners just voting Labour in the north; they should also 'phone their friends, their sons, their uncles and aunties, people who had been made economic refugees from their own homeland and had gone south to settle in Surrey and London, and get them to vote Labour in their new constituencies. 'Blood of your blood,' he said. 'Flesh of your flesh. Bone of your bone.' In other words, nothing of any consequence.

But it wasn't what he said that mattered; it was the way it was all done. Here was the new leader with his new ways. First of all, before he appeared, the warm–up band was very lively, playing a medley of *Pagliacci*, 'Rule Britannia', and 'I Dream of Jeannie', modulating into Dixie when the local bigwigs made their entry. Then Mr Kinnock appeared. He hadn't much cared how he dressed before, but that night he wore one of the dark blue suits that were to become so familiar. He made his entrance alone, and with his hands held over his head. And his entrance was accompanied by a stirring and romantic and undoubtedly caring bit of something that sounded familiar, rather like a bit of Beethoven rearranged to make a best selling pop single out of it: a good strong tune. When he had finished, he made his exit to the same symphonic accompaniment. I slunk over and asked one of the bandsmen what it was: he didn't know, but

several of his colleagues put their heads together and decided
that it was very likely a bit of Brahms's First Symphony.
And it was. When I next had the chance, I asked Mr Kinnock
about it himself. Had it been his own idea? 'Yes,' he said,
'and one day I'm going to have it played by the LSO on a
party political broadcast.'

Well, there it was, the Kinnock style revealed. All that
remained to be added was the red rose. All that remained to
be dropped was the red flag. Mr Kinnock says that for him
the colour of liberty is red, but he and advisers got rid of a
great deal of it, relying instead on sky blue for the background cover of pamphlets, and a sort of beige for the
party's podiums and platforms.

At any rate, there at the start of the election was Mr
Kinnock, three years on from Newcastle, wearing the same
style of suit, making the same entrance to the same Brahms,
and punching the air with that same confident gesture of the
upraised arm. 'What you see', he said of the manifesto, 'is
what you get. That is our democratic contract with the
British people.' As the campaign got going, it became obvious that the contract as presented lacked a lot of the fine
print – on defence, on taxes, on the unions – and each time
something new came out it did Labour no good. But in the
Churchill auditorium that morning, Mr Kinnock was in
high humour.

'Everything's coming up roses, then?' he was asked. He
was happy to agree. His foes would be delivered into his
hands.

What about the Looney Left, though? What had changed?
Insofar as such people were even fringes, said Mr Kinnock,
they were tassels hanging on the edge. They had no influence, no importance, and we'd best spend the next few
weeks ignoring them. A question about tax was then evaded,
and then Mr Kinnock and Mr Hattersley – standing together
on their podium with four window boxes of roses and ferns
in front of them – were photographed holding the manifesto
up high, together, just as the child Amy had been held high
and made much of the day before. No other member of the

the Shadow Cabinet, not even Denis Healey, got a word in throughout. The presentation was an imperial performance. Even when it came to questions Mr Kinnock dominated, and I made the final score Kinnock seven, Hattersley three, everyone else nil.

But this was, incidentally, the day that the other parties conceded an essential precedence to the Conservatives. Without a numbered, laminated pass with your colour photograph on it you got nowhere near Central Office, or any Tory meeting or politician. Applications for these passes were vetted by Special Branch. The passes – and there were at least four different kinds conferring different degrees of access and privilege – then had to be worn hanging round the neck on metal chains. It soon became clear that the other parties were not even trying to do anything similar. The Alliance did issue yellow bits of cardboard on request, with no picture or checking required, but I was never once asked for mine and never used it. Labour for its part never entered the unequal contest, issued no passes of its own, and happily accepted the Tory pass.

But even with this pass, it took forty-five minutes to get into Central Office for the launch of their manifesto. Every bit of the photographers' equipment was checked, though what the check showed was not clear. The public could just walk into the Conservative shop, which had been moved into a Portakabin a few yards from the front door: it would have been as easy to plant a bomb there as buy an 'I love Maggie' teddy bear, price £2.95, or one of the several picture postcards of the leader offered for sale, or the little blue fluffy gremlin-like creatures, all eyes and two white paws, with a large distinct streamer at the front saying 'Support the Conservatives' and a small and indistinct legend on the back saying 'Not to be sold as toys'.

Now the Tories organize things like fêtes and elections very well. That is the widely held prejudice. It is also the experience of many years. But it was obvious from the beginning that that morning was going to be a shambles. People were brawling to get in. When they got in there was not nearly enough room. It is a small hall which has served well enough for the last several elections, but there were four new London newspapers this time, each with two people there, and above all there were more photographers. Photographers in the pack, particularly foreign photographers, are a curse. Those from the London pop papers are cunning, resourceful, and a blight on the land wherever they go. They nevertheless have a finesse which their French and Italian colleagues somehow lack. Ten minutes before the launch was due to start, they were standing three deep in front of the platform, that is when they were not attempting to climb over each other. 'Can everybody', pleaded a Conservative girl trying to keep order, 'please keep their hands off the platform. It gets dirty very quickly.' No notice was taken of her. Three minutes before the Prime Minister arrived the better part of the Cabinet – or the better part minus one – filed in and sat down. This was what the IRA would have loved to get at – Baker, Young, Younger, Lawson, Whitelaw, Tebbit, Howe, Hurd, Fowler, and Ridley all in a row. Then Mrs Thatcher took her seat in the centre.

The Central Office staff attempted a hopeless deal with the cameramen. Would they care to take as many pictures as they liked, and then depart? Would they like three minutes? Four then? Four and a half? Forty photographers took not a blind bit of notice, and carried on taking pictures, not one in a hundred of which could conceivably be used. I saw no one leave.

The reporters waited.

'No music this time,' said Mr Adam Raphael of 'Newsnight', making notes. 'Last time it was "Rule Britannia".'

'"The Dambusters",' said Mr David Dimbleby of BBC 'Election '87'. 'Why are you writing all this down? Are you going to do the trivia?'

'No Biffen,' said Mr Raphael, surveying the line-up of ministers through the mob of photographers. 'We all ought to invite him on to our programmes.'

There was indeed no music at all this time, and no Biffen

either, even though he was the Leader of the House and Lord Privy Seal.

After five minutes, when it seemed that the photographers had at last finished for the moment, Mrs Thatcher made an uncharacteristic error by remarking that perhaps some of them hadn't got a shot, at which half of them swarmed back again.

Then at last there was near silence. Mrs Thatcher said that the manifesto was a weighty document in all senses, not something that had been dreamed up behind the doors of smoke-filled rooms. 'We are', she said, and the mere proposition took everyone by surprise, 'a team. Ask my ministers questions.' Then a pattern emerged. A question would be asked. She would then reply herself, at length. Then she would say, to a question on the health service, 'But Norman, you should be saying all this.' And Mr Fowler would add something. Or on defence: 'I'm sorry I didn't hand this over to George. I will in a moment. George, would you like to put it very much better?' At which Mr Younger would have to mutter a form of words indicating this was, of course, hardly possible.

There were nuances to be observed in the way she addressed her ministers. Mr Lawson was addressed by her as Chancellor of the Exchequer; Mr Hurd as Home Secretary; Mr Fowler as Norman; and Mr Ridley as Mr Ridley. But what this meant was not clear. Was a man in greater favour if he was addressed by the Prime Minister by the name of his high office, or by his Christian name?

Sir Geoffrey Howe answered a question on South Africa. 'How diplomatic you are,' she said. But at any rate it was not a one-man show as the Labour launch had been. Members of the Cabinet, unlike those of the Shadow Cabinet, were not required to sit in a row like mute witnesses in an esoteric play put on by a heavily subsidized theatre. There is no way Mrs Thatcher can fail to dominate anything, but at my count the top scorers among her ministers were Mr Hurd with six replies and Mr Ridley with five. Mr Tebbit, although not invited to respond, managed two interjections.

Yes, but what, she was asked in the end, had happened to Mr Biffen? 'We are pretty full,' she said. He was not one of the ministers responsible for any of the main aspects of the manifesto. Well, the Leader of the House wouldn't be, would he? But from that moment the fate of John Biffen was sealed. He should never have been so indiscreet as to have mentioned, the year before, the virtues of a balanced leadership.

But would he be appearing at subsequent press conferences? He was not, said Mrs Thatcher, responsible for a department. That too was true – he was not Education or Health or Transport or the Treasury, just Leader of the House, responsible for seeing the government got its business through. Anyway, he was done for.

Mrs Thatcher ploughed on. The hacks were dropping with the heat. 'She will', said Mr Raphael, after almost an hour, 'exhaust us all.'

FOUR

Billiard Room to Jockey Club

It was in the largest billiard room in the British Empire that the Alliance leaders showed their great displeasure with Mrs Thatcher. This billiard room is in the basement of the National Liberal Club in Whitehall Place. The club itself, in recent political history, has stood as an ever diminishing symbol of a shrunken Liberal Party. When it was opened in 1884 it was the largest club in London, with the most members, and Gladstone was Prime Minister. Seven prime ministers – Gladstone, Rosebery, Campbell-Bannerman, Asquith, Lloyd George, MacDonald and Churchill – were among its members at one time or another, the last two having been elected when they were Liberals. The club's architect, Alfred Waterhouse, was the Victorian architect par excellence. He was also the creator of Manchester town hall and Salford prison. He created in Whitehall Place a building of grandeur. Even the lavatories were the most splendid in the British Empire, lined like most of the building with faience, glazed encaustic tiles.

But since the beginning of the '70s the club's decline has been pitiful. The splendid library was closed and the books sold or given away. The great dining room was hacked into two bits. The terrace facing the Thames, one of the summer glories of the club, was more often closed than not. Its awnings grew ragged. Bad fitted carpet was laid over hardwood floors. Solid original furniture was replaced with modern rubbish. The old club servants died off or left. The tiled pillars in the great rooms were coated with emulsion paint. Sir Neville Cardus, the great cricket writer and music critic, who had lived at the club for years, found somewhere else and took himself off. The *Guardian* moved its annual literary prize-giving from the club. Liberal Members of Parliament had traditionally stayed there when they were in London, but there were now few of them. The club then let rooms to foreign students, at least to those who were willing to put up with having only one bathroom to each floor. Because the lift from the hall to the bedrooms frequently failed, these interlopers, most of them apparently Scandinavian girls, often took a short cut through the smoking room, disturbing the few members who still attended. Gladstone's axe, with which he was supposed to have chopped down trees in his old age, disappeared from over the mantelpiece. Then the bedrooms were sold off to the hotel next door. The two bits of the dining room were reunited, but otherwise all was dismal. Redecoration was in progress, but the glory was gone.

Even the famous lavatories were diminished. These were lavatories with a history. F. E. Smith – though in his later incarnation as Lord Birkenhead, after he had become Lord Chancellor – used regularly to pop in and visit these lavatories, though he was Tory. This was noticed, and a brave club secretary one day stopped him and enquired whether he was a member. 'Oh,' said the great man, 'it's a club too, is it?' There is some doubt in the mind of historians whether the club in question might not have been the RAC or even the Athenaeum, but F. E. Smith's latest biographer has demonstrated that the National Liberal Club lay on the Lord Chancellor's likely daily route: for myself, I am sure the tiled grandeur of the Liberals' lavatory, as well as that club's political inclination, clinches the matter.

By the time of the 1987 election the lavatories and the adjacent washrooms had been recently reduced to a quarter of their former size. The antique balancing scales where members could weigh themselves were gone. Even the box of shoe brushes was gone. And set up on the site of the famous loos was the Alliance shop, selling manifestos and political geegaws.

The only splendour left to the club was the portrait in the hall of the young Winston Churchill as a Liberal Home Secretary before he crossed the House and joined the Tories. And, strangely, the billiard room survived. And its pillars had escaped the emulsion paint slapped around elsewhere, and glowed gold in the television lights.

On the platform were David Steel and David Owen, both indignant that the Conservatives, having in their manifesto said that Labour's unilateralism would lead to a neutral and fellow-travelling Britain, had added that the Liberals and Social Democrats would take the nation more slowly down the same disastrous road.

David Owen had written to Mrs Thatcher protesting. In the billiard room David Steel spoke first. As ever, he said, she seemed quite unable to apologise or admit to error. From the patronizing and bossy tone of her letter, you might think she was trying to treat the Alliance leaders as members of her own Cabinet. He would not have Liberals traduced as fellow travellers. The First World War coalition had been led by a Liberal. In the Second World War the then Liberal leader had been responsible for the RAF. Well, this was all true. But to hear the name of Lloyd George invoked, from seventy years back, was a bit odd. For Mr Steel to resurrect the name of Archibald Sinclair, which though from more modern times is quite forgotten, was even odder.

But Mr Steel was very angry. He had tacked the bit about the two Liberal leaders on to the prepared text of his intended statement. 'For her to slur my party as fellow travellers', he said, 'is a disgrace.' Mr John Cartwright, the Alliance spokesman on defence, then said Trident was a Rolls Royce defence system. Britain did not need a Rolls Royce. It needed a Maestro. This made you wonder if he could ever have driven a Maestro.

Dr Owen then sadly remarked that he had written to Mrs Thatcher as Prime Minister and that she had replied as Leader

of the Conservative Party. Which led us into the second spat
of the morning. Over at Smith Square there was another
dispute about who had said what and who should reply in
what capacity to whom.

Mr Tebbit, as Chairman of the Tory Party, was snarling
at Bryan Gould, who was officially 'co-ordinating', but
appeared to be running, Labour's campaign.

The details are tedious, but, briefly, Labour had run an
advertisement quoting Mr Tebbit as having said, four years
before, on radio, that if unemployment was not below three
millions in four or five years' time, then he would be 'not
worth re-electing'. Mr Tebbit said he hadn't said it, and
wrote to Mr Kinnock challenging him to produce a transcript or a tape, or else be shown up in a blatant lie.

Mr Kinnock did not reply. It was Mr Gould who wrote
back to Mr Tebbit, co-ordinator replying to chairman,
giving the date of the broadcast. But if you read between
the lines it was plain that Labour hadn't got a transcript or
a tape.

Mr Tebbit then wrote furiously back, not to Mr Gould
but to Mr Kinnock:

Dear Neil Kinnock,
This morning I wrote to *you* challenging *you* to justify the
words *you* attributed to me in *your* advertisement in the
Daily Mirror today.
You have failed to do so.
You offer no evidence at all.

And so on. The recurring word *you* was fiercely underlined
by Mr Tebbit's pen.

Once again it was Mr Gould who wrote back.

Dear Norman,
Thank you for your further letter to Neil Kinnock. I have
already given you the date and place of your comment.
We are too busy to indulge in childish games. We are
fighting an election – what are you doing?

Now before the election little was known of Bryan Gould – ex-Balliol, ex-diplomat, ex-reporter on 'TV Eye'. But he was making a golden reputation. He was cool. He kept his cool. He even appeared to be more familiar than some of his more senior colleagues with his own party's proposals. He was a good chap. But he obviously hadn't got a tape. Then suddenly he had, and he called the Press together to hear it played. Back to Transport House, where this time the photographers were being firmly asked to go:

'Are there any snappers in the house? You'll have to take snaps and then go.'

'Don't call us snappers. Snaps are what you take to the chemists.'

Then Mr Gould explained that the resources of the Labour Party should never be underestimated, and produced a girl called Rosie who happened to have found a tape in a cupboard . . .

'Over to Rosie Brocklebank. Er, Brocklehurst; sorry.'

The momentous tape was then played. On it, Mr Tebbit didn't say he would not be worth re-electing, but that he didn't think the Tories 'would be in a position to win the next election'.

The loop of tape as played contained sixty-three words and lasted probably twenty-five seconds.

'Is that all?' [Sceptical titters.]

Mr Gould said it was, but intimated he could find more.

And the tape had been stuck in a cupboard for two years? [Amusement.]

Mr Gould made light of this.

Mr Ian Aitken, political columnist of the *Guardian*, then asked: 'Settle for a draw?'

Mr Gould declined this offer, at which he was told from the floor that at that rate both he and Mr Tebbit might be warned off by the Jockey Club. Then things went back to normal. A question was asked about how much more tax people would have to pay under Labour, and an evasive answer given.

Afterwards, on the way to Sloane Square, a cab driver

asked me if I knew about this MP, Vivian Bendall, Conservative of course, who was a consultant to the London taxi drivers and had a picture of a taxi on his election leaflet, and also did a lot of work for Soviet Jewry. Throughout the campaign, cab drivers talked of nothing but politics. The driver of cab 8012 was no exception. 'I vowed', he said, 'when I became a cab driver, I'd never discuss politics, or religion. Now I've done both.' He said his wife would vote Alliance regardless. As for him, he thought Owen and Steel had really got the needle to each other. 'So, better the devil you know, which is a terrible thing really. You've got to worry about your income first.'

And of course, as the honest-as-the-day-is-long Bryan Gould had known, when he fudged that last question on higher taxes, the only party solemnly promising such higher taxes was Labour. He undoubtedly knew also that the last man to make such a daft promise was Walter Mondale, in 1984, and look what happened to him: he took one state, and the District of Columbia, against Reagan's forty-nine.

FIVE

The Undoubted Leader and Mrs Pugh's Pies

The election was a week old when Mr Kinnock went down to spend two days in his own constituency. Those two days, and one event which preceded them, told the story of the way he saw the leadership of the Labour Party, and how he was setting about being leader – and God help anyone, opponent or colleague, who didn't understand.

The night before the trip to Wales, Labour produced the single most memorable event of the campaign that far, and it happened on television. Of all unlikely things, a Labour election broadcast was a hit. It was a great deal more than that. Nothing like it, or approaching it, had ever been seen on British television.

Party political broadcasts are usually kept to five minutes, though a party can have ten minutes if it wants that much. But it was generally thought a feat of great daring to try and keep an audience's attention for five minutes, let alone ten, so ten was rarely attempted. The Labour Party did attempt it, succeeded marvellously well, and, in showbiz terms, established Neil Kinnock as a bankable name. From then on, if he were an actor, his face would have been recognized, his services sought, the best parts offered him, and scripts sent round to his agents on spec, in the hope that he might read them. He would get his name above the title. Not, as it were:

LABOUR IS GOOD FOR YOU
with Neil Kinnock

but rather

KINNOCK
in the award winning
COMPASSION

There in this party political broadcast was Mr Kinnock walking with his wife Glenys. Then Kinnock to camera saying the real purpose of power was to help others. Then Kinnock on his father, and on his valley. Then the camera panned over a still black and white photograph of the young Kinnock with his mother and father, with the Kinnock voice-over: 'Both of my parents died . . . within a few days of each other. That – was a shattering experience, but I had this immense good fortune of having Glenys, and of Stephen, who was nearly two years old, and Rachel was born a week after my mother died. And, as human beings do, you have to pick it up and get on with it. And I know that my parents' instinct would have been to say, "Give yourself to the next generation. Think the best things of us, and remember us, but get on with life, because life goes on."'

Then Kinnock in close-up, Glenys in close-up, their son and daughter in close-up, then another still of Mr Kinnock's parents, then Mr Kinnock and Glenys walking, and then sitting on a cliff edge, and the theme music of Brahms everywhere in the background, swelling and then fading. Then Kinnock working late in his House of Commons office, with its Pugin panelling and furnishings, and light from a green-shaded lamp.

Then came the play within the play. 'The Expulsion of the Militants' said a caption, and then there were television

clips of Mr Kinnock, at the party conference at Bournemouth two years before, denouncing the grotesque chaos
of a Labour council, a *Labour* council, hiring taxis to scuttle
around a city handing out redundancy notices to its own
workers. Cut to the villain Hatton in the body of the hall,
yelling abuse. Cut to Kinnock on podium. Cut to hall
applauding, cut to Kinnock, cut to hall. The Militants were
seen to be routed in thirty seconds. Then cut to Mr John
Smith, Labour's more or less unknown trade and industry
spokesman, who has, however, an honest face full of gravity, saying it had taken real guts for Kinnock to do that. Then
a clip of Mr Healey, and then one of Sir James Callaghan.

Then away from mere politics and back into Kinnock
singing in a choir, and so on. Now at the first time of seeing
I just smiled at the play within the play, and then watched
the rest. After that I played the video several times, and the
play within the play became a bit dubious. I remember
Bournemouth well, but to call it the Expulsion of the
Militants is a bit much. No one was expelled that day or for
a long time afterwards, and then precious few. And to say,
as John Smith did, that it took real guts for Mr Kinnock to
put it as squarely before the party as that, is going too far:
Kinnock should have said it a year before, and, even in
saying what he did when he did, he never even mentioned
the name of the city where the taxis were scuttling around.
He never said it was Liverpool. As to the Healey shot, he
compared Kinnock to Gorbachev: 'He's got a nice smile,
but he's got steel teeth.' That's a back-handed one if you
like: anyway, you could say the same of Mr Healey, the
civilized old thug – which is something he admits of himself
in his more confiding moments. As to Callaghan, he could
out-trim Kinnock before breakfast, and knows it, and what
was the viewer to make of his saying that Mr Kinnock might
be young and inexperienced, but that the same had been said
of 'William Pitt, you know', in the eighteenth century, when
he became Prime Minister at the age of twenty-five. Mr
Kinnock is forty-five, only a year younger than Pitt was
when he *died*.

But then back to Kinnock, and his wife – whom he called warm, intelligent and loving – and then Kinnock talking about his ancestors and asking why he was the first Kinnock in a thousand generations to be able to get to university? Was it because they were all *thick*, these people who made beautiful things with their hands, and dreamed dreams, and saw visions? Was it because they were weak – those people who could work eight hours underground and then come up and play football? Weak? Those women who could survive eleven childbearings? [Close-up of Glenys.] Were they weak? No, it was because there was no platform on which they could stand, and, as he said this, the word Labour tracked slowly across the screen. It was the only time Labour got a mention in the whole ten minutes. More Brahms, more Kinnock, more Glenys, a gull soaring, and then at the end the single word 'Kinnock' on the screen.

It was magnificent. It was difficult not to break into applause at the professionalism and audacity of it. A political party had produced ten minutes of film which were not only watchable but gripping. No harm in a laugh at the double-edged teeth of Healey and Callaghan. No harm in reflecting that only thirty generations of Kinnocks would take us back to 1066, and that to go back a thousand would land them in the stone age. It was entertainment, something no party broadcast had ever achieved before. More than that, when Mr Kinnock was talking to camera about his parents he was utterly convincing. The director, Mr Hugh Hudson of *Chariots of Fire*, had created another bankable name, and demonstrated, incidentally, that Glenys Kinnock was a natural.

So much for the television campaign. As for real life, word was getting back that Mr Kinnock out in the country was hardly speaking to reporters at all, and not that much to the public either, only to television cameras. Well, we should see. I was due to travel down to Wales to spend a couple of days with his circus there.

At 7.10 the next morning, at Paddington station, the Menzies kiosk was still not open, though you could buy newspapers if you wished, and nothing else, from a stall in front of it. The *Daily Mail* was leading on Labour's secret tax plans, having calculated that everyone earning over £15,340 a year would be paying more – about five million people, that is, hardly the 'super rich' whom Mr Hattersley had said he wanted to mulct. Elsewhere, Mr Healey was reported to have compared Mrs Thatcher to Stalin. Normal.

Miss Hilary Coffman, from the Labour Party, had seventeen of the Press to look after, and, in the dining car of a very crowded train, found them all breakfast. Distinctly displeased businessmen were turned away hungry because of her block booking. Now to remember to feed the Press breakfast may seem one of the more trivial political virtues, but it isn't. I had known the Labour Party for years, and this was the sort of thing they were likely to get wrong. Historically, it's Labour that holds its rallies in filthy cinemas a foot deep in litter and fag ends, and it's Labour that forgets to feed its own candidates, let alone the Press. Things had changed. Miss Coffman herself was a big change from the traditional run of Labour Party minder. She knew what the programme was and quietly did her damndest to see that everything worked. She provided tickets where tickets were necessary. She soothed anxieties, provided minibuses to take people up mountains, and gave straight answers to straight questions. All this with the lovely assurance of the English middle-class woman. And she was, remember, dealing with the Press, which Labour traditionally loathes, and which Mr Kinnock deeply distrusts. She just got on with things. She will not like this, but I think the best way to give an idea of her is to say that at Conservative Central Office, where they habitually do these things well, she would have shone.

Wales seems from London a far-off place of whose people we know nothing, but the train was in Newport in an hour and a half, and on the bus to take us to Sirhowy the photographers were already making requests for photo-opportunities. Could they have Neil Kinnock, together with a rugby player, and a miner?

Miss Coffman: 'With a lamp?'

Mr Kinnock had not come down on the train with us. He and his wife liked to spend as much of the campaign together as they could, and went back to their house at Ealing most nights. They had driven down to Wales that morning.

Mr Kinnock's constituency used to be Bedwellty, but was renamed Islwyn in the redistribution of the early '80s. That made it the only British constituency to be named after a poet. Islwyn (1832-78), otherwise the Revd William Thomas, started life as a surveyor, then became a Methodist minister, and turned to poetry after the death of his fiancée. He won several Bardic crowns. There used to be pits here, but they all closed in the 1960s. Now there is countryside, round which we travelled at length. All the reporters from the pop papers had Cellnet telephones, on which they constantly telephoned stories to their newspapers, stories which were practically never used. One of the older hands put his Cellnet to better use, telephoning three bookies to get the best odds before putting £30 tax paid at three to one on Real Moonshine at Pontefract.

We met the Kinnocks half way up what looked to an Englishman like a mountain. He was about to open Sirhowy Valley country park. There he stood in the rain in his statesman's clothes – dark blue suit with red rose – declining offers of a mackintosh, when even Glenys wore one. There were sheep around, and a mayor, and photographers.

'Gentleman with the chains,' commanded a cameraman, 'could we ask you to step aside so that we can get Glenys in?'

A ceremonial tape was cut with sheep shears. Mr Kinnock, still in statesman's clothes, walked further up the mountain where only zoom lenses could follow, and then he walked down again and presented conservation badges to twelve Cubs. Having done this he gave a three finger salute, explaining that each finger stood for one million unemployed.

To the left rose one wet mountain. To the right, across a valley, was another, covered with Japanese larch. We were not above the tree line, but the Londoners were impressed by Mr Kinnock's hardihood in getting up that far and then leaping up and down precipitous slopes. The local inhabitants were not. As a man from the Countryside Commission put it, 'If Nixon can walk the great wall of China, Neil can do this.'

Then we all went back down the mountain to find the little town of Pontllanfraith. The red door of 28 Sir Ivor's Road was pointed out. This was the Kinnocks' terrace house in the country. It was pointed out to everyone, and was conspicuous because of the single policeman on the door. Then we went to a pub called the Penllwyn Arms for lunch.

The best bar was crawling. It looked as if the locusts had descended. I went to the empty public bar next door and ate. From the best bar came a ferment of noise and then a crash, and then yells. A table had collapsed under the weight of a television crew clambering on top of it. After a while I went in and looked, and there was Mr Kinnock surrounded.

'Welcome to civilization, Mr Coleman,' he called out, having caught my eye across the crowded room, and he bounded forward and I barged my way through the mob, and we shook hands with great warmth and then sat down to discuss the state of the election and Mrs Pugh's meat pies.

This was strange. I have never called him a new Aneurin Bevan, and as I've said he hadn't been talking to reporters all week, only to television cameras. Perhaps this reluctance had become important, and something had to be done about it, when it became so noticeable that it was itself reported in television, as it had been. But perhaps it was also that he had had an undoubted triumph with his broadcast – which by then was being talked of as *Ecce Homo* brought to you by the director of *Chariots of Fire*. Or perhaps it had something to do with his being in his own local pub in his own constituency. He praised Mrs Pugh's meat pies. He had asked for one but there were none left because they had all been eaten by the television crews. He said the pies were wonderful. Mrs Pugh worked at the pub and did lunches. He often popped in for one.

Who was the Sir Ivor after whom his road was named?

Sir Ivor Markham, he said, a mining engineer who became a pit owner. The house would have been built for a pit foreman at the turn of the century.

What about Mr Ken Livingstone, who had been reported as saying seditious left-wing things about the leadership? 'He's now saying he didn't say it.'

He had talked to Mr Livingstone? No, he hadn't, not himself, but that was what he was told.

Still, there were plenty in his party who were well to the left of himself, weren't there? 'Tassles,' he said amiably.

The broadcast had been very polished, hadn't it? He agreed it had, and said Hugh Hudson would do another one for him.

It had a strong story-line, hadn't it? 'The story of my life.'

A bit American, though? 'Not really. Professional, yes. I've always been irritated by second-rate methods . . . But I don't want [here he simulated a voice of deep and perhaps American evangelical sincerity] any of this Here's a Man of the People sort of thing.'

He thought the campaign was going well? 'After 1945', he said 'we had twenty-five years of being casual.' The way he said this showed there was going to be no more such sloppiness.

But that broadcast again, which incidentally hadn't even mentioned that there was such a thing as an election on, hadn't it ended with just the word 'Kinnock' on the screen, and a red rose? 'That was Hugh Hudson's idea. I would have put "Labour" and the rose, I guess.'

Still, wasn't it a bit presidential? 'My conception of Labour has always been as a movement, not just a party.'

An American reporter then asked him about conference decisions not being in the manifesto, and Mr Kinnock good-humouredly gave what he called a WEA lecture to explain things: conference decisions didn't have to be included, only considered for inclusion, and so on. So there he was chatting, and whether he liked the man-of-the-people idea or not he had taken the trouble to change into man-of-the-people clothes, having swapped the dark suit of that morning's mountaineering for a sweater and slacks. And then one of Mrs Pugh's famous pies did arrive for the leader, and he ate it. All good human stuff.

Then that afternoon we were off to meet Mr and Mrs Jenkins at Twyn Gwyn farm, near the hamlet of Man Moel, near Blackwood. It was a long and narrow one hundred acre farm, another two hundred acres having been taken long before by British Coal and the Forestry Commission. It is called a hill farm, but I'd say it perched on a mountain, and the name says just that in Welsh, in which language it means White Farm on Top of a Mountain. As the borough of Islwyn's glossy brochure says, these steep slopes remind us of times when travellers, wary of wild beasts and unfriendly natives, cautiously made their way along ridge tops uninhabited except perhaps by skylarks and sheep.

That afternoon, seven television crews and about ninety hacks in all made their way along a ridge 1,200 feet up and warily regarded wild beasts like merino ewes and mares and foals. Mr Peter Jenkins, celebrated political columnist of the *Independent*, in a pinstripe suit and a Garrick Club tie, carefully patted two baby lambs. A huge rabbit glowered from a cage. Patricia Hewitt, Mr Kinnock's sparky press secretary, she who sent him the well-leaked memo about the dangers of the Looney Left and the London Effect, exclaimed on the beauty of a stallion. Mr Kinnock posed holding a shepherd's crook in one hand and Angharad, a child of the farm, by the other. From the yard, a sheepdog of the farm surveyed the circus with glances of rapid intelligence, working out how to get some order out of the chaos, how to shed the politicians and pen the press. Then the circus backed up and left. Sheep went Baaa.

Later, in the town of Blackwood, Mrs Kinnock opened a new branch of the Citizens' Advice Bureau. She and her husband are close. She has always had a great influence upon him. When in 1970 he was first adopted for the very safe seat of Bedwellty, as it then was, he appeared before the selection committee wearing his wedding suit, as she had insisted he should. He won the nomination by a majority of one vote. Earlier, when they first met at University College, Cardiff, he was campaigning for Nelson Mandela and against South African oranges. When they married, it was Glenys who insisted that, having made a fuss about the oranges, they could not buy a ring made of South African gold. So they bought one made of Scandinavian silver. Before the general election there was much speculation that she was some way to the left of her husband, and that this would appear in the speeches she would make. Labour was anxious to scotch this rumour. In Blackwood it was put about by the party's press people that this would be the only speech she would make during the entire campaign.

Then there was a parade down the High Street, but to get out of the rain I went straight to Mr Kinnock's committee rooms, where I was hospitably given a Welsh cake and a cup of tea. While I was waiting I looked at the Neil Kinnock 'victory' mugs, on sale at £1. These mugs had a Union Jack on the side, and Mr Kinnock's head in the middle of the flag. They reminded me of a mug I was once given at school to celebrate the coronation. Then a woman ran in from the street calling out, 'The cameras are coming. We can't have cups of tea in here with the cameras coming in.' The cup was whipped from my hand, and Mr Kinnock entered with attendant television cameras. 'Hi kid,' he said to a constituency worker, slapping him amiably about the face. 'All right?' This was a frequent Kinnock gesture of friendliness.

The ITN crew bought three of the £1 mugs, though what Labour's tax proposals would have done to their salaries was awful to think of. Patricia Hewitt was standing outside for a bit of peace, still talking about the stallion of Twyn Gwyn. I said she was very taken with the beast.

'I used to ride a lot.'

'What, stallions?'

'No, but it's such a beautiful horse.'

As we all left, Kinnock victory mugs were given away free to the Press, which did not please the ITN men who had earlier parted with their money.

Between the events of Mr Kinnock's day there were long
drives through countryside, and that evening we landed up
at a dismal greystone Victorian hotel with uninterrupted
views of more countryside and, to the astonishment of an
American reporter, only one usable telephone line, which
was already being used. Miss Coffman explained gently to
him that he would appreciate this did happen in some remote
places. Here the Pontnewydd Male Voice Choir (est. 1904)
was singing to entertain a visiting delegation from the
People's Government of Guanxi Zhuangzu Autonomous
Region, in China. The idea was to twin Gwent County
with the autonomous region, Gwent and Guanxi Zhuangzu
having common interests in pig-breeding and cultural song
groups. When I arrived the choir was taking a break and, at
the special request of the seven Chinese visitors, a woman
soprano was singing 'Home Sweet Home'. Then the choir
sang the theme song from *Exodus*, the film, with words
about a land where children could run free. Mr Kinnock
joined in a song called 'Llanfair'. He sang first base but was
professionally pronounced to be really a bottom base. I
asked members of the choir what 'Llanfair' meant, but they
insisted there was no acceptable English translation. Mr Ken
Allen, a redundant steelworker, told me the words were
appropriate to Neil Kinnock. He produced the sheet music
and asked me to note two lines:

Saints within his courts below
Praise him, praise him, evermore.

'Now what about that?' asked Mr Allen. I said it appeared
to be about God, didn't it?

Mr Allen: 'To us, if we're going to speak about Neil, he's
our God.'

All right, but what about the Shadow Cabinet then?

'They're his saints below, aren't they?'

Mr Fred May, another of the choir, a retired fitter, then
told me that his grandfather was killed with 440 others in a
pit explosion of 1913. 'Four corpses in the same house,' he

said. He showed me his hand. It was injured when he was eighteen, and he got £75 compensation. This sum was then stopped from his father's dole. He said the same sort of thing was happening today: he had saved when he was in work, and now, because he had some savings, he got less in benefit. 'And as for the pension, I worked fifty-one years of my life and she gives me twenty pence a week rise . . .'

Mr Zhang Chun-Yuan then made a short speech. 'Back home,' said Mr May, 'I've got a little red book of Mao Tse-Tung. There's very few of them around.' Mr Kinnock then made a long speech.

Afterwards, I tentatively asked Mr May, 'What if Mrs Thatcher wins again?'

'God bless her,' he said, 'may she go down in history – six feet.'

Then he said: 'I get by, but sometimes it's a struggle. The drinks are free for the choir tonight. Otherwise I couldn't drink at all on my pension. The boys won't drink much, though.'

I thanked him. He said: 'I hope I haven't overpowered you?' The choir went on singing till late, 'Jerusalem' and suchlike. Mr Kinnock sang with them.

There was then another mighty drive back to a pretentious Ladbroke's hotel at Newport. It offered adult films in your room – *Fanny Hill*, *Vanessa* and *The Pleasure*. The instructions were set out in a folder which showed on the cover the representation of a girl sitting on a bed and either taking off her stockings, or putting them on, according to taste. You selected Channel 8, pressed the 'confirm' button, and £3.95 was automatically added to your room bill. It is an American idea. The rooms were good, of a decent size, but it was a hotel which was quite uncomprehending when it was expected to serve food after ten in the evening. There was said to be no call for it. When, after some insistence, dinner did appear, the food was indifferent to bad. Mr Peter Jenkins, having carefully chosen the wine, pronounced it to be industrial effluent and declined to drink it. That was hyperbole, but this was a hotel where the bill for a single room and dinner came to £74.84, in South Wales. It was no grand hotel, but a rather lavish motel. It was imitating the American style, but I have never found a motel anywhere in deepest America where the coffee shop was not open all day and until late. Next morning, breakfast was served to the sound of muzak. And when we came back for lunch the next day, which was a Saturday, we were told that lunch was not served at all. The staff could not have been friendlier, but they really did not understand why a pack of reporters and cameramen were so put out to learn there was no lunch.

But never mind the hotel, which was only one in a long line which had turned out to be in one way or another dim. The fact was that Kinnock was on the up. After the singing of 'Llanfair' that evening, and the earlier climbing of mountains, all was sweetness and light for him. A good political day.

★　★　★

Next morning early, Mr Kinnock was in Cardiff launching the Welsh campaign and the Welsh manifesto – Maniffesto Llafur. This time the title on the cover was Buddogoliaeth i Cymru (Wales Will Win), but the exultant photograph of Kinnock on the front cover was the same.

He appeared on a platform with only three officials, and not one of the nineteen Welsh Labour MPs. It was a one-man show again. He said Wales had been battered by Thatcherism, and that a Conservative government would not resist the selling off of coalmines. He did not suggest who would want to buy them.

Then came questions. In London, the day before, Mrs Thatcher and her Education Secretary, Kenneth Baker, had put forward differing interpretations of Tory education policy. It had seemed, anyway, that some schools would be able to take the brightest pupils they could find. This is heresy to a socialist, and Mr Kinnock said it showed Mrs Thatcher's scrap-book mentality. He meant that in her eyes the child of ordinary ability was so much scrap.

What was he going to do with the Militants who (despite 'The Expulsion of the Militants') were still in the party, some of them parliamentary candidates? He said 'due process' was necessary.

But what about Mr Livingstone (not a Militant) and others like him? His mutterings were now more than rumours, and had been widely and circumstantially reported. Surely Mr Kinnock couldn't go on dismissing such people as tassels? He replied that those who had any other form of separate manifesto would not at any time exercise influence on the leadership, the direction, the strategy, or the policy of the party. He added for good measure that the Press had brought itself into disrepute by its partisan reporting of remarks made by such people, to do mischief to the Labour Party. This was such nonsense, and nonsense that had been trotted out so often before, the same old ritual bit of abuse, that nobody took any notice. The newspaper which had the most substantial report on Livingstone that morning was probably *The Times*. No one wasted any breath pointing out that there was likely to be more than a grain of truth in such a long story, since Mr Kinnock detests Rupert Murdoch's *Times*, and, in public at least, seemed convinced that every member of its staff had sold his soul to Mr Murdoch for thirty pieces of silver.

Then a reporter asked a good question. He said that five years before, at Ealing Town Hall, he had heard Andrew Mackintosh, then the moderate Labour Leader of the GLC, give much the same assurance (about extremists) as Mr Kinnock had just given. He said the similarity was uncanny. A few days later Mackintosh had been deposed by Livingstone.

The reporter then went on: 'Nobody doubts your sincerity . . .'

At which Mr Kinnock was at him. 'Don't patronize me, son.'

It did not sound pretty.

The reporter tried to continue: 'But don't you think the voters fear the same thing could happen to a Labour government as happened to the GLC?'

Mr Kinnock went for him again: 'You're a political reporter, yes? Let me introduce you to a few considerations. We
don't elect a leader of the Labour Party in the same way that
group leaders (of councils) are elected. Second, there's the
question of my attitude towards the leadership of the Labour
Party, and that will continue. Thirdly, I think the kind of
scenario you paint may make for a mildly interesting novel,
but it bears no relationship to the realities of the politics of the
Labour Party or the conduct of a Labour government.'

That was that. He would take no more questions, and
left.

Oh Lord. Back to the rough house. And the reporter at
whose throat he had leapt was not a serpent from the *Sun*
but a political correspondent of the Press Association, Mr
Jon Smith, who had been following him all week, whom
he perfectly well knew, and whose copy was straight. The
Press Association is not a member of the universal Press
conspiracy against Labour. Now the PA man was young,
so Mr Kinnock could just about call him son if he liked.
And perhaps it would also be more prudent in a reporter
not to tell politicians that no one doubts their sincerity. But
the fact was that Mr Kinnock could have made the same
reply with good humour, and he hadn't. For a moment or
two he quite lost his cool, and it looked awful.

Back in the bus the reptiles of all political colours put their
heads together and compared their notes, and checked them
against a tape recording of what he had said. That was the
extent of the conspiracy that morning. 'Silly,' said a woman
reporter. 'We'd have gone on education otherwise.'

Mr Kinnock then went on to a display of martial arts at
a youth club – karate, kick-boxing and judo. The young
members had twenty-six black belts between them. Over
the judo wrestlers hung a legend reading Ren-zu-kai, which
means Spirit of the Warrior, and presiding over the hall was
a picture of Gunti Kozume, a great warrior of the eighth
Dan, who was said to have committed hari-kari back in the
'70s. Nobody knew why. 'Perhaps', said Mr Kinnock, 'I
can come back some time and get some instruction, because

in my game sometimes I could do with it.' The general opinion among the following Press was that he could look after himself pretty well.

Outside in a corridor Miss Hewitt came up and asked me not to make too much of the stallion thing. 'Just a couple of lines,' I said.

In the afternoon, there was the ritual cavalcade around the endless hills of Mr Kinnock's vast constituency, a car with balloons flying, a yellow bus broadcasting its never-ending bit of Brahms, then a yellow Land Rover pickup with Mr Kinnock and his wife standing in the open back, then the Press, then half a mile of cars.

After half an hour we passed the photographers' bus which had got lost and, in trying to catch up with us, was travelling rapidly in the opposite direction. They were late because they had refused to budge until they had at least had a few sandwiches for lunch.

It rained. 'Last time,' said a woman reporter, 'we were at the Commonwealth Prime Ministers' conference by the side of a pool in Bermuda, and now it's come to this.'

Labour press girl: 'This is the people.'

Still it rained. Past the Mount Zion chapel we went, and the Coal Hole Inn, and the New Ko Sing chinese restaurant, and the Miners' Welfare Hall, through grey streets but, for longer stretches, through valleys between wet hillsides. Mr and Mrs Kinnock still stood in the open in the rain, he shooting his arms up, punching the air with that triumphal gesture, for all the world like Mayor Koch of New York going down Fifth Avenue on St Patrick's Day; only this was a rural Koch, punching the sweet damp air, and often with more sheep than constituents to watch him.

It was meant to take three hours. After two the Press was mutinous and wanted to get back to London. Only one woman reporter, terrified of the wrath of her news editor, refused to peel off and leave the parade to its own devices. She urged upon us that nothing should be thought impossible since that man got into the palace and sat on the Queen's bed. What if Mr Kinnock were assassinated after we had deserted him? What if there were an Armalite in that next clump of trees?

'Why not,' asked the quiet and rational voice of Mr Andrew Gimson, representing that most entertaining of political weeklies, the *Spectator*, 'why not assassinate him now and get it over with?'

The single-mindedly conscientious girl was ditched, our bus eased over a sheep grid which the more intelligent sheep were said to render useless by curling themselves into a ball and rolling over it, and we set out for the motorway and Newport.

On the way I re-read the often checked notes of that reply of Mr Kinnock's. The bit that really mattered was the sentence in which he said: 'Second, there is the question of my attitude towards the leadership of the Labour Party, which will continue.' Which meant, being interpreted, 'I'm the boss, and I'll stay boss.' It accounted for his imperial campaign, his brilliantly folksy party political broadcast – which was really a commercial for himself – and for everything. He had said, incidentally, that there was to be another TV broadcast made by the *Chariots of Fire* man, and the feeling was that it could only be known as *Kinnock II*. All in all, he was on the up and up. Even the lost temper of that morning, which was no news to anyone who knew him at all well, would do little harm to a man who, much as he might proclaim the need to care, needed also to be feared a bit. He was doing much better than most had imagined. The party organization was working, and, much more important, he had established himself as undoubted leader. This was not something that even a couple of weeks before could have been taken for granted. The common political talk, in the days before the election was called, was that the knives were already out for Kinnock, that he would lose and would then be not so quietly got rid of. It was not turning out that way at all. His opponents of all parties, and particularly of his own, would be wise never to forget his toughness, and his ruthlessness. Patronize him, as it were, and you end up in one of Mrs Pugh's meat pies.

The flying Press, anxious to get back to dinner parties or just away from the sodden land of the poet Islwyn, reached Newport just in time to see the Inter-City 125 for London easing out of the station. There was an hour's wait. On the London platform, in the men's lavatory, there was a filthy towel, no soap, and no hot water. In the waiting room, one of the Labour press relations girls was still carrying the shepherd's crook presented the day before to her leader.

SIX

A Critical Situation
in Salisbury

'No way,' said the man when Edward Heath, out canvassing, offered his hand. 'No way. My name would stink.' Mr Heath is not usually associated with such violence. He is a more complex man that that. It is true that he detests Mrs Thatcher, who superseded him as leader, and calls her 'that woman'. But only the most diehard opponent could hate him. He is regarded by some with affection, and by others with mistrust. Most of all, perhaps he is regarded with incomprehension.

Mr John Biffen – than whom it would be difficult to meet a saner or more charitable man – once told me that when he came into politics he had two heroes. One was Edward Heath and the other Enoch Powell. 'I would say that both are now pretty well as far away from my present political patch as I could very well imagine, but whereas with one I can still enjoy a tremendous rapport, and a genuine respect, with the other, it's a glacier.' It was with Mr Powell that he still had the rapport, and Mr Heath who was the glacier. And there is Mr Hurd, now Home Secretary, who was Mr Heath's political secretary from 1970 to 1974. He always admired and respected Mr Heath, and remembers sides of him that others don't. He recalls Mr Heath's taste for early morning champagne before 'those ghastly press conferences' during the campaign of 1970. He saw, remembers, and continues to admire Mr Heath's subtle diplomacy with the

French, with the Chinese, and with 'those very special gentlemen', the princely leaders of the Gulf states – with those, in short, who might be thought the most prickly or exotic, and the most difficult to get on with. When he went to the Foreign Office himself he emulated this tact. And yet, as he also remembers, when he once wrote a short history of the Heath administration (a fair and friendly account, too), Mr Heath thought it trivial, and did not trouble to conceal this opinion.

For my part, I had the good fortune to get to know Mr Heath on the eve of his victory in 1970. I also happened to be there when he was on the edge of failure in the second election of 1974. His message on that second occasion was that the nation faced ruin and anarchy, but his campaign lacked lustre and all he roused was apathy. During a general election, time is precious. Moreover the election of October 1974 was one on which he knew his political life depended. But he spent a large part of one evening in a club which was not even expecting him, because the club president had not bothered to tell the members he was coming. He attempted an interview with Canadian television but the lights failed. After much persuasion, he unwillingly tried his hand at snooker and failed to pot a red, which he should have hit much harder. Then at eleven at night, with a few days to go to the poll, Mr Heath – who had earlier that day made a speech saying there were times when things fell apart – stood with a few advisers in the dark forecourt of an obscure club in an obscure suburb. 'Any ideas?' he asked, and if there was any immediate reply I did not hear it. The little group just stood there by his car.

Nowadays, he deserves his reputation as a proud man, but that is not a deadly sin. He can be bitter, but he has cause for that. His pride shows itself in silences, and his bitterness mostly in shrugs. I have seen him passionate on the ideal of One Nation, in which he believed with his heart and still does, and have also heard him speak with passion – though he will not thank me for using that word – about a greater thing than One Nation, about what he calls the snapping of a generous international tradition, which existed from Marshall onward – a generosity whose great international exemplars were Churchill, Monet, Averell Harriman, Paul-Henri Spaak, Willy Brandt. It is a generosity which he believes has now been abandoned, principally by nationalistic Americans like Mr Reagan and by Mrs Thatcher. Now, he says, it is every nation for itself, and he hates the meanness of it.

By last June, Mr Heath had just failed to be elected Chancellor of Oxford University, and had recently conducted a concert in Peking which had raised $800,000 for charity. His reputation abroad was greater than here in Britain. He was living for the most part in his newly acquired house, part fourteenth century, part late-seventeenth, in the cathedral close at Salisbury, but went about the country doing more than his share of electioneering. I followed him in two strangely contrasting constituencies – scrubby Hornchurch and prosperous Chelmsford. The strange thing was that the first was safe for the Conservatives and the second highly marginal.

Outside the Constitutional Club in Hornchurch, the Conservative candidate and sitting member, Mr Robin Squire, who is an accountant, stood in a downmarket blue windcheater and described his downmarket constituency: fifteen per cent of families worked at Ford's Dagenham plant, and seventy-six per cent owned their own houses. He said it hit you between the shoulder blades, or should he say between the eyes, that it was true-blue working class. Well, so it may be, but until 1979 it was held by Labour and it was one of those seats Labour had to take if it was ever to form a majority government again. Yet the Conservative majority was 9,184.

And why was Mr Heath coming to Hornchurch? 'An old friend,' said Mr Squire. He thought many people would not even know of the rift between Mrs Thatcher and Mr Heath. 'To ninety-five per cent of people he's still a recognizable figure in the streets – like Heseltine. He's a father figure.'

The father figure arrived on time, having driven up from

Salisbury, and straight away turned into Mr Heath the old pro, showing that he could work a crowd, and press the flesh, as well as any man. He was in and out of a Wimpy bar in a minute flat, having received the promise of two votes for the candidate. The manager of Sainsbury's, though wearing a Rotary badge, was reluctant to let the canvassers and cameras inside his busy supermarket, and asked if they could just go in very quickly. The candidate, with a timorous bonhomie, said they mustn't spoil the business, mustn't interfere with the money making. Mr Heath walked in with assurance.

Just inside the door he came across a man whom Mr Squire identified as an opponent. 'Ah,' said Mr Heath, extending his hand. 'No way,' said the man, with real bitterness. He was the one who said that to shake hands would make his name stink.

Near a special offer of British chicken at 46p a pound, Mr Heath was himself asked which party he belonged to and how he proposed to vote. Mr Squire explained, saying, 'We don't get too many ex-Prime Ministers, do we?'

Well, no. Mr Heath was about the only one around. Lord Home had appeared at the opening rally in Scotland, but had otherwise taken little active part. On the Labour side, neither Lord Wilson nor Sir James Callaghan, whose wife was ill, was able to do much.

On the pavement, Mr Robin Squire gave away favours, in the shape of a robin, saying 'Vote for Robin.' Inside Molly's Florist, 'Cars' were 25p a stem. Cars were carnations. Mr Heath was presented with two cars specially dyed blue for him. Outside, a scruffy man in sandals, who said he was a headmaster, asked Mr Heath to put in a word for education with the Prime Minister. Perhaps he could do that? Mr Heath passed a shop called Cordon Bleu – special offers baked beans 22p and Kellogg's Frosties 95p – where he was yelled at by an irate pensioner. Then he glanced in the window of the Topcat Discount, which dealt in fancy goods and kitsch, and then returned to the club to meet local businessmen.

None turned up, so Mr Heath sat at a table, drank black coffee, and talked to me about the twenty-first century and this one. Mr Heath, as elder statesman, habitually takes the longer view. 'People talk to me about the next century. We've only got twelve and a half years to the next century. You can't build industry, or change industry, overnight.'

No. I then remarked to Mr Heath that his name did not occur once in the index of the *Campaign Guide*, which is the fat reference book about policy and recent political history put out by Conservative Central Office at election time. 'Well,' he said, 'it's what has happened ever since the leadership changed. An attempt has been made to obliterate me from the history books, and certainly from public life.'

How far had that attempt been successful? 'You can see that it's bound to be unsuccessful. You saw going round the streets this morning. Everybody recognized me and greeted me cheerfully, and so on.'

I asked him why there had been riots in the last few years, when in the 1930s, with just as much unemployment, there hadn't been. First, he said, there was really less unemployment in the '30s, and in those days there were only marchers, like the Jarrow marchers, who were solemn and serious. Only later were there demonstrations. Then came television. Riots all over the world could be seen on the screen every night. Then there were riots here.

But he did not despair of the present? 'I don't despair, but I think one has got to recognize the obvious fact that young people who have nothing whatever to do, do start despairing, and they lose the capacity to work. And they have energy. They're going to find some means of releasing that energy.'

Smashing things up? 'Yes. We are very lucky it hasn't been worse.'

Michael Heseltine appeared to have adopted his views, then? 'He was in my government.'

What could you do about a derelict Sheffield, whose steel no one wanted any more? Take Liverpool, he said. This was a city that had been created by shipping, by merchants, by entrepreneurs, by commerce. The men who created the city's trade also created its art galleries and its splendid buildings. They lived in the city themselves. Then in the 1930s the Mersey Tunnel was built. The merchants then went and built pleasant houses in Cheshire. The city was deprived of its leaders. The same thing happened later in Birmingham. So should we try to bring these people back to the inner cities? He thought this would be unlikely to work.

The candidate appeared and told us about the man who had declined Mr Heath's hand in Sainsbury's. The two of them, candidate and indignant man, had worked together on a hospital project in the town, so they knew each other, but the man was solid Labour. If there were two men left voting Labour in Hornchurch, he'd be one of them. Mr Heath was charitably assuming that the man had simply not wanted to be seen shaking hands with him in front of cameras. I wasn't. The ring of true and cherished intolerance is unmistakable.

Then the candidate's wife and a woman friend came into the club. The friend was from Exeter. 'Why aren't you working in Exeter?' asked Mr Heath. 'The whole of the west is being swept away in a total avalanche.'

There was silence.

'Plymouth will go,' he said. 'Bath will go.'

At this there was uneasy laughter from the candidate, because Bath was marginal.

'Taunton', said Mr Heath, 'will go.'

More uneasy laughter, because that would have been a disaster.

'If you were down there,' he said to the woman, 'you could save it all.'

Glances were exchanged. Mr Heath then decided to enjoy himself. 'We have', he said, 'a critical situation in Salisbury.'

Salisbury?

Don't repeat this, he said, but the house next to his had been let to a multi-millionaire. And he had received a letter from this new tenant, saying, 'Dear Mr Heath: We are now neighbours and I hope we'll soon become friends. I have been adopted as the SDP candidate for Salisbury. If at any time you should have any difficulties, particularly of a political nature, I hope you will not hesitate to contact me so that I may try to resolve them for you.' [General laughter, and heaves of Mr Heath's shoulders.]

Mr Heath departed for Chelmsford. I was in the club lobby at Hornchurch, trying to telephone when the candidate's wife swept out past the candidate. 'That', she said, 'is the last time I come here for you.'

Chelmsford, thirty miles north-east of London, is hardly in the same country as Hornchurch. It has the river Chelmer, greenery, a cathedral, and two grammar schools, and had been until the dissolution of the last parliament the seat of Norman St John-Stevas. But his majority in 1983 was only 378. He had been run close by the Liberal/Alliance candidate, who was standing again. It was a constituency where Labour would be lucky to get five per cent of the vote, but which the Conservatives might fail to hold.

The new candidate was Simon Burns, young, an Oxford man, founder of the Rutland Young Conservatives, once political adviser to Sally Oppenheim, and until the election a conference organiser for the Institute of Directors. After a light lunch of paté, sandwiches, and plonk, he gave assurances that the defence policies of a future Tory government would not harm Marconi, who employ 9,000 people in his constituency, and that tactical voting for the Alliance wasn't going to happen on his patch because it had already happened in 1983. If you looked at the Labour vote, which was down to nothing, you could see this was probably true.

Mr Heath was asked if comprehensive schools would disappear under the Conservatives. He said No, and then inserted this quiet barb: 'Mrs Thatcher created more comprehensive schools as Secretary for Education in my government than any other Education Secretary has ever done.' Comprehensives had gone wrong simply because they were too big. Headmasters couldn't get to know the staff, let alone the children.

'What about the Arts?' he was asked. Should there be more money for the arts?

Now the Arts are always an issue of sorts, since those who don't get grants endlessly claim that they should, and those who do endlessly claim they should get more, and assert, year after year – without it ever once occurring to them that it would be a neat solution if they were to offer just this proof of their recurring assertion – that if they don't get more they will have to close down. It is also safe to ask Mr Heath about the Arts because he loves music. So should the arts get more? 'Yes. After all, Norman St John-Stevas was Arts Minister in my government.'

What if subsidies were withdrawn? 'Then the so-called working class will pay a little less tax, but if they want to go to the opera they will have to pay the full price. I can't accept that. Where would Mozart have been without the Archbishop of Salzburg?'

The candidate then said Chelmsford was the third fastest growing city in Europe – though he couldn't name the first and second – and we went out to have a look at it, Mr Heath saying that this was his twelfth general election campaign.

The High Chelmer shopping mall is as prosperous as any you might find in the flusher suburbs of Detroit or in any German city. It has high glass arcades, of the sort there used to be three of in Bournemouth before they went out of fashion and were allowed to rust. A fashion boutique took American Express and Diners. The flower stall was a real stall. The Harvest Bakery sold six kinds of bread rolls. 'Super, super,' said the candidate, whenever anyone promised a vote. The candidate's wife, red-headed, douce, with little black bows on her shoes, followed a few paces behind. Her name was Emma. She said she and her husband lived in the constituency but that she worked mainly in Wiltshire and Gloucestershire. She found the M25 a godsend.

What did she do? Interior decorating, she said; mostly curtains at the moment.

With which firm? Colefax and Fowler.

Ah. How exact. Her husband's was a Colefax and Fowler constituency.

In the arcade, one woman told Mr Heath she was a widow and found it hard to bring up a seventeen-year-old son on her pension. Two young men hung around and were closely watched by Mr Heath's detectives. When they did eventually approach it was only to tell him they were on holiday from Winchester College and to ask if he had any plans to visit Winchester. Mr Heath's bodyguard consisted of two detectives, one in crocodile shoes. There were also eleven uniformed policemen at a discreet distance. That was as many as he had when he was Prime Minister. Indeed, I never remember seeing so many uniformed police with him then. Times are thought more dangerous, even in Chelmsford.

Mr Heath was then steered to a shop calling itself The Life House. It sold natural cosmetics, herbs, little bags of roasted buckwheat, and books on dietary matters. He looked at an earnest rack of books.

'I must say it's all very frightening – *Brittle Bones and the Calcium Crisis*. It all sounds a bit like Westminster.'

Frightening it may have been in Chelmsford. The toasted buckwheat vote was surely, by its nature, solidly Liberal/Alliance.

Outside The Life House Mr Heath was accosted by a man who said: 'We had a meaningful talk in Dunstable, fifteen years ago.'

'Ah,' said Mr Heath.

'About the dollar, which was then at 2.78.'

After a few warm words about the days when £1 was worth $2.78, Mr Heath had a few other words with his young private secretary about how to get back to London to put on his tails. He was due to give the address at a memorial service in St Paul's cathedral that afternoon for Sir George Thalben-Ball, a great organist recently dead at the age of ninety.

It was the most English of occasions, a celebration rather than a memorial, with Sir George's colleagues, friends, admirers, and pupils gathered under the dome, and American tourists for the moment kept out – though if they said they wanted to join in the service or listen to the music they were let in, and shown to seats by ushers in morning dress.

First, there was a Bach recital – the Toccata, Adagio, and Fugue in C-major, and 'Now thank we all our God', and other pieces. Then came the service. One of the lessons was the parable of the talents, in the Authorized Version, and this is a parable which should bring it to mind that in the early days of his own administration, before he turned to incomes policies, Mr Heath was very much a free market man, and in that sense a precursor of Mrs Thatcher's policies, long before she was much heard of.

It was thought that Mr Heath would speak from the lectern, but he was shown into the great pulpit. He spoke about the splendour of the music we had heard, the brilliance of the organ playing, and the purity of the singing. He remarked how Sir George had never been attracted by baroque tendencies but had always celebrated the English tradition of church and cathedral music, and recalled his own days as a boy chorister. As a young man he had bought a gramophone record of the Thalben-Ball recording of 'O for the Wings of a Dove', with the boy soprano Ernest Lough. It had sold more than a million copies, more than any other classical record. Mr Heath said he had last seen Sir George at almost the last recital he gave in Salisbury cathedral. He had first met him in 1954 on the liner *Windsor Castle* on passage from Cape Town to Southampton. In the fourteen days they were thrown together they talked mostly about music, though Thalben-Ball sometimes showed a rather querrulous interest in politics. Sir George was a man who loved good food and good wine, a wit, a man of wisdom, and a man who gave dignity to any gathering.

Well, the organ recital before the service, by the American organist Carlo Curley, was of a brilliance I have never before heard. Spontaneous applause rang through the cathedral. And this was not an occasion divorced from the political Mr Heath. This was just another face of the only British Prime Minister who was ever organ scholar at Balliol. And when he spoke about that record he had once bought, I recalled another occasion, almost exactly seventeen years before, on the eve of the 1970 poll which he won but which he believed, even to the end, that he had lost. It was late at night in the headmaster's study of a grammar school at Bexley, in his own constituency. Mr Heath was alone, without his aides, and without his Central Office girls, who had all gone home. He poured himself half a tumbler full of whisky, drank some, put it down next to the headmaster's mortar-board, and for the first time that day forgot to sit up straight, and for the first time let his suit sag around him. Mr Heath was the first British Prime Minister to campaign in the American style, changing his suit and shirt and tie two and three times a day so as always to look crisp and new. Then he saw I hadn't got a drink, poured me half a tumbler too, and asked me what I wanted.

I asked some question about a biographer who had attribute to him a deep sense of religion and a belief that he was a man of destiny. Was he? He was too dead tired to give a daft question the sharp answer it deserved. He mumbled something I couldn't catch, said after a while that the man who had talked about his feeling for destiny hadn't seen him for thirty-five years, and then went on answering yes, no, or mutter.

Mr Heath was also the first party leader to carry his own platform with him at elections, a set that was carted round and set up afresh in each hall. That year, his had blue concentric circles on it. What did they mean?

'Nothing,' he said. It was for the benefit of the television cameras.

He allowed television to dictate such an important thing as the symbol on every platform of his? 'Why is it important?' he asked. I said because his head was going to appear in front of it in hundreds of photographs. He said it was

designed so that the television lights would bounce off it on
to the speaker.

The interview was not thriving. I was getting him to say
hardly anything at all, just 'Yes,' or 'No,' or 'Obviously.'
It was fair enough. If a man is tired, and you haven't the
wit to ask questions that draw him out of his shell, that's
your look-out. Then, quite by chance, I asked a last question,
about something he had said in his speech that night. It was
a question that showed I had not understood, and he told
me so.

But he had said that the key to everything was the creation
of more national wealth? Was that really the key to everything?

'Yes.'

'Without exception?'

'Without exception.'

Then he came alive and spoke with a direct strength I
hadn't seen in the two days I had been following him. 'If
you've ever been poor', he said, 'you will know that.'

Not, he said, that he had ever been really poor, but
freedom did need a certain amount of money. 'Look, the
joy I've had today, seeing these young people (there had
been many at his Bexley speech), they've got an immeasur-
ably freer life than I ever had.'

How? 'Music. They buy LPs I could never afford . . .
Never until my second year at Oxford did I buy a record.
Without some prosperity you can't have a full life; travelling,
theatre, books, books of your own and not borrowed from
the library. I never bought a book of my own until I was at
Oxford. This matters to me. I like to have things of my
own. Pictures of my own, even if they are poor pictures. If
you want freedom, a life which can be active and reflective,
then this (enough money to go round) is the basis.'

I objected that there must be, and must have been, poor
societies which were happy. He agreed, and I was saying
'Thank you, Mr Heath,' and preparing to leave, when he
stood up himself and talked with something that sounded
like passion. It had been a joy to him, that last week, when

he was travelling, to see everywhere that there were young people enjoying these things. He did not, as I understood him, use the word 'joy' as a politician would use it from the platform. He used it as a word one doesn't use often, and it was very surprising. He said it wasn't just materialism. He wasn't just talking about that. Once before, when he had talked about the joys of life, the former Archbishop of Canterbury had written asking if he didn't mean just having a good time, and he had replied, 'No, I don't.'

But weren't friends, women, children, among these good things of life? He said of course they were, but let him tell me, you were a damn sight more capable of enjoying something if you didn't have to worry about not having enough. 'There's an old saying of the Salvation Army: "You can't cast out the devil on an empty belly." And they're right.'

That was all seventeen years before. Within a couple of days he was Prime Minister. Defeat may change a man in many ways, but not in all. The man who had spoken that afternoon in the cathedral about his record of 'O for the Wings of a Dove' was the same man who had spoken, late at night, over a glass of whisky, about wealth, and freedom, and the key to everything.

SEVEN

Devonport, and the
Time Has Come

The Holiday Inn at Plymouth has an extraordinary view, overlooking the sea and the Hoe from which Drake sailed to beat the Armada in 1588. If Drake did play bowls before he sailed, it would have been more or less on the site of the hotel. It has a restaurant on the top floor which is called The Penthouse in Springtime. From the restaurant you can see ancient cannon pointing out to sea, and memorials to the dead of this century's two world wars. On the menu the hotel is written down as The Holiday Inn, Plymouth, England, which is unnecessary since there is no Holiday Inn at Plymouth, Massachusetts. The evening I was there most of the diners were American. The waitresses said there were three parties of them, ninety in all, and that there was a sort of two-way tourist shuttle. Some Americans visiting England came first to Plymouth and then made their way northward to Edinburgh. Others started in Edinburgh and then travelled south, ending in Plymouth. It was a pleasant hotel, the best I stayed in throughout the election, though not the grandest or most pretentious. The waitresses spoke as I remember my grandmother speaking. Plymouth is altogether a most English city. Like London it was heavily bombed in the war, and still has some of the scars. Where you find a car park, it was a bomb-site. But the air is fresher than London's, and life is slower. Some big English cities are now in parts so mixed that it is strange to enter one like

Plymouth, where there are no more black faces to be seen than there were in the late eighteenth or early nineteenth centuries. Perhaps fewer, because there were many blacks in Nelson's navy.

Plymouth, Devonport is Dr Owen's constituency. The boundaries have been changed over the years. The division has taken in the council estates of north Plymouth, which ought to be solid Labour but are rather more solidly Owen-ite, and has lost parts of Devonport. But it's no surprise that to any member for Devonport the Navy should be something special. It's not only a matter of getting frigate refitting yards built there to give work to his constituents. Because he is the member for Devonport, and because he was Foreign Secretary under Callaghan, there was only one way David Owen could have responded to the Falklands invasion. He has said so. He believed that what was at stake throughout the war was much more than Mrs Thatcher's neck. What was at stake was Britain. Had the war gone wrong, the repercussions of seeing General Galtieri celebrating the first anniversary of the invasion would have been great. It would not just have been that our international credibility would have been diminished. It would have been, but one could have lived with that. But he believed that, within the country, the Little Englanders, the people who believed that Britain should behave as if it were a small Scandinavian country, the unilaterists, the neutralists, the pull-out-of-NATO people, would have been much encouraged. To have lost, or not to have fought, would have been demoralizing.

I have some connection with Devonport myself. My maternal grandfather, Frederick Grose of Truro, served in the Royal Navy from 1884 to 1919. The names of the ships he served in – *Impregnable, Agincourt, Royal Adelaide, Vivid, Revenge, Sans Pareil* – are a splendid litany from the years of the Pax Britannica. He was one of the first naval divers. In his long career he served all round the world. He was once on the China station. He remembered shore leave in San Francisco. He retired as a petty officer and joined the Coastguard. He was a great reader, borrowing half a dozen books a week from the public library. In his later years he was a Labour man, and took the *Daily Herald*. He gave me my first dictionary, which I still use, though it is now in rags. It is bound in red rexine, and I believe he won it from the *Herald* in one of the circulation wars of the 1930s when newspapers gave away sets of Dickens rather than bingo prizes. My grandfather died at the age of ninety-one. When we came to look at his papers we saw that as a boy he had falsified his age to enable him to enlist two years younger than the law allowed. When he lay dying, and was delirious, he kept on saying he had to get back to Devonport to rejoin his ship.

★　★　★

It was half way through the campaign when I went down to Plymouth with Dr Owen. The Alliance had shown no sign of breaking any moulds. In the beginning, the Conservatives had considered that Labour would tear itself apart, and that the real threat would come from the Alliance. Before the election date was announced, the Alliance had been catching Labour in the polls. But by mid-election it was plain that nothing of the sort was happening. The Alliance's fast start has shown itself to be a mistake. The two Davids had been flying round Britain together in their executive twin jet for several days before the other parties did anything. The two of them, photographed endlessly together in the cabin of this little plane, looked rather odd. So did their television interviews together. They were called Tweedledum and Tweedledee. The joint television interviews were abandoned. Owen and Steel took off on their own separate campaigns, meeting most days for an evening rally. But the Alliance ratings in the polls obstinately stuck at about twenty-one per cent.

Theirs was the most frenetic campaign. Mrs Thatcher gave herself several light days. Mr Kinnock did not bother to start his days with London press conferences. But Dr

Owen and Mr Steel were holding theirs together nearly every morning, and then departing, each on his separate tour. On one typical day, David Steel went to Battersea, Hereford Marsh, Brecon barracks, Shrewsbury, Wrexham, Liverpool, and then back to London that night: David Owen, that same day, went to Stevenage, Hatfield, Luton, Manchester, Bolton, and Liverpool, and then also came back to London. Another day, Dr Owen was photographed, in the presence of Concorde, with an SDP candidate who happened to be a Concorde pilot. That day Mr Steel had to make do with a walkabout in a Jaeger knitwear factory.

The day that Dr Owen went down to his own constituency in Plymouth started with the usual joint press conference at the National Liberal Club. Downstairs in the billiard room, after the obligatory music on the loudspeakers, which that morning was a bit of Tchaikowsky, Mr Simon Hughes, the Alliance spokesman on health and on Church of England affairs, was holding forth on health. Mr Hughes is the Liberal who unexpectedly won Southwark and Bermondsey in a lucky by-election of 1983. The constituency Labour Party was in ruins. Mr Bob Mellish, who had been Chief Whip under Harold Wilson, and was also a papal knight, had become so alienated from the party that he resigned. The constituency then lumbered itself with the unfortunate Mr Peter Tatchell, who was crucified, and, after one of the dirtiest by-elections in memory, lost to Mr Hughes. Mr Hughes then held on to his seat in the general election of 1983, and made a reputation as a diligent radical pest at Liberal conferences.

In the billiard room he sought to illustrate the length of the health service waiting list by unfolding an unending computer printout of names and letting the folds of paper drop from the platform on to the floor. Cameras busily photographed the falling swathes of paper.

Mr Hughes then somehow got himself into a mess by remarking that only the first names were real. The rest were symbols.

Mr Paul Johnson, the most rigorous of political writers, and a man with a keen nose for the spurious: 'It's a fake?'

Mr Hughes then got himself into a worse tangle by trying to explain that the names weren't real because confidentiality had to be preserved.

Jeers. If confidentiality had to be preserved, what about the bearers of the few real names?

Mr Hughes then insisted that whether names were real or not wasn't relevant to the debate, just their number.

More jeers, and groans.

That was let drop, and Mr Steel was asked how the general campaign was going.

Mr Steel said they were not fortune-tellers, but they both thought things were going well. Dr Owen went one better. Very well indeed, he said. As this thoughtful campaign continued it was becoming a thinking person's election. There would be a late surge to the Alliance.

There was no apparent evidence of either thoughtfulness or of any such surge. Dr Owen was asked if he wasn't a bit puzzled. He said he wasn't. It was just that the class nature of British society tended to solidify during a general election. The Alliance was freeing the mould.

Um. What about the problem of having two leaders? No problem, said Dr Owen. People had got used to the two Davids. He thought it a considerable attraction. To which Mr Steel added that a poll had discovered that three-quarters of voters liked having two Davids.

Those present trooped out to the two buses waiting in Whitehall Place. There was, throughout the campaign, a careful distinction of name. Mr Steel called his a battle-bus. Dr Owen, who was a bit contemptuous of that name, called his a campaign bus. The two buses were given these separate names on the daily programmes which showed where the two men were going. The programme was on a single sheet of paper divided by a vertical line down the middle, with Dr Owen on the left and Mr Steel on the right.

On Dr Owen's bus we set off for Surbiton, one of the
least populous constituencies in England. It is solidly Tory,
used to be Sir Nigel Fisher's, and that morning's informed
speculation was that the visit must have been arranged as
long ago as the time Rosie Barnes won the famous Greenwich by-election, when there were sanguine expectations of
an Alliance landslide. The SDP candidate, Mr Tom Burke,
rose up in the bus and gave an address with bull-like energy,
saying that the Alliance now controlled the local council and
that he was an environmentalist. Yes? Did that mean he was
a unilateralist too? He denied it, saying the two didn't always
have to go together.

We arrived at Surbiton. These days never mind the man
on the Clapham omnibus. Outside Chestnut Cottages, circa
1890, Dr Owen sniffed yellow roses and chatted with the
biochemist in the Surbiton street. Several of his colleagues
had been braindrained, and he had been tempted himself.
You could see that Surbiton had come up in the world. The
streets around were full of what had been artisan houses,
now going for £70,000. Several had mock-Georgian doors
and Quality Street bow windows.

Then on to Carshalton, another safe Tory seat, which
used to be Robert Carr's when he was Home Secretary.
There Dr Owen emerged from the side door of his bus. The
bus bore a legend in huge letters, saying 'The Time Has
Come.' The door opened just where the 'e' came in Time.
He then toured a college of further education, wandering
among lathes, presses, and drills, asking searching questions
of boys who were learning to repair cars by the useful
method of restoring ruinous wrecks. 'Once did a week's
course myself', he said, 'on how to keep a Land Rover
going.' But it was a college which also offered full-time
courses in Hairdressing and Beauty Studies. You can tell
things are getting high-flown when hairdressing is not called
hairdressing but hairdressing studies. And the beauty studies
offered instruction not only in manicure and pedicure but
also in psychology and journalism, which is subsidised nonsense. And on a notice board, the University of Sussex,

which ought to know better, offered a part-time MA degree in 'Women and Education'. Gender, it said, was now recognized as a crucial factor. Another poster said Jesus was the Answer.

It was a college where many of the teachers were disaffected. 'I ♥ Teaching But I'm Tired of Subsidizing It', said another poster. Perhaps the staff *were* subsidizing it. The lowest-paid lecturer there was on only £5,910 a year and the highest-paid on £14,000. The average was about £10,000. The mechanics and hairdressers they train would get more than that.

When we were on the bus once again, Dr Owen asked me whether Mr Heath had really said those words about an avalanche sweeping the West Country. I said he had, but that exactly what he meant by them was another matter. We travelled on to Gatwick, went through the plentiful but sloppy security of the VIP Winston Churchill suite, and boarded an old prop-jet Avro 748. Leaflets in the seat pockets said it was owned by a 'third-level' airline that was in turn part-owned by a company which also had sixty sea-going tugs. On the short flight to Exeter everyone wanted cold salmon rather than quiche for lunch. The ITN girl nicked a third-level airline lunch and two bottles of airline wine to take away. Dr Owen said he would be making the most of Mr Kinnock's two gaffes – talking on television about the 'occupation' of Britain and saying Labour would restore to unions the right of secondary picketing. As we lurched into Exeter airport, he was still chatting to reporters and had to be implored back into his seatbelt, but not before he could also impress on us those issues like defence and the police, on which there was no longer a bipartisan policy – 'Tripartisan, I should say.'

His little plane was the largest at the airport. Cows watched it taxi in. Dr Owen disappeared in a car, saying all hell would break loose if he was late getting to his constituency. His campaign coach followed on more slowly, down narrow lanes bearing advertisements for the Devon County Show. That evening there was the big rally at

Plymouth Guildhall. Dr Owen's election leaflet, a copy of which was placed on each seat, was resolutely parochial. 'Everybody,' it said, 'knows somebody who has been helped by David Owen.' He was described as having brought the dual carriageway to Plymouth, having pushed forward the building of the Derriford Hospital, having opened that frigate refitting complex, and having recently opened Toshiba's brand-new second factory in Plymouth. The leaflet also quoted the *Western Evening Herald* as calling him statesmanlike, and the *Sun*, of all the London papers you could choose, as calling him engagingly honest. A second, smaller leaflet, added that he was widely tipped as the next Prime Minister.

His entry into the hall was a triumph. A Purcell trumpet voluntary announced him and he came in with his American wife Debbie, who launched him up on to the platform and then glowed with love as she watched him from the front row. There is a lot to be said for American political wives. David Steel was there too, and presented Dr Owen to his own constituents as 'Your David, our David'. He explained that he had had trouble getting into Plymouth in a fog. His helicopter had got lost. It had just avoided the spire of Buckfastleigh church when his pilot asked Plymouth to bring him in by radar. To which the reply had been that they didn't have radar at Plymouth. However, he was there, and was soon on form, condemning the harsh and spivvy world of Margaret Hilda Thatcher, and seeming to quote Gladstone in describing himself and Dr Owen as 'fellow soldiers in a common warfare'.

Mr Steel might call Gladstone in aid, but it was Owen, when he came to speak, who looked like a Gladstonian statue, right leg forward, left hand extended to the lectern. He started off reading out the words of Mr Heath which I had reported a few days before, about that avalanche in the west. We were in the west, but I don't think most of the audience knew what the point was. The expected applause and laughter didn't come. Perhaps Dr Owen's supporters in Plymouth didn't know that Bath could possibly fall to the SDP, or that if Taunton did, as Mr Heath had suggested, it would mean that their man was well on his way to a say in government. I'm sure that second point wasn't taken.

Dr Owen then went straight for Kinnock. 'Secondary picketing rules, OK?' he asked, and went on to Mr Kinnock's admitted support for it, which hadn't been in the manifesto. Cat now out of the bag, he said: police handcuffed; streets handed over to Scargill's and anybody else's private armies; and so on.

Those two speeches put the difference between the two Davids in a nutshell. Mr Steel went for the spivvery of Margaret Hilda Thatcher, Dr Owen for the fecklessness of Mr Kinnock.

All the Alliance rallies throughout the campaign were on the same lines. They were all called 'Meet the Alliance', and, after the opening speeches, written questions were invited from the audience. These rallies were open to anyone who cared to walk in. This was very different from the other parties', which were all-ticket affairs. The Tories could not help this: there was no way they could let a casual IRA man walk in from the street. For Labour there was no excuse at all, but Labour doesn't like heckling these days. It is thought irreverent to heckle, which, when you think of the state of constant uproar in which Labour conferences are habitually conducted, is strange. Anyway, heckling was not encouraged at rallies.

'Ask the Alliance' was getting on well at Plymouth that evening when the master of ceremonies arrived, very late. This was Mr Bamber Gascoigne, a celebrity, whose fame is that he is famous for being question master on 'University Challenge', on television. He was late because his helicopter had also been diverted, in his case to Newquay. He took over and rapidly created a deeply-felt wish that he had been diverted to Land's End, making such a facetious meal of whether the written questions handed in were from Miss or Mzzz, or from Mr or Mzzz, that David Steel, having had enough, told him he was sex-obsessed. To which Mr

Gascoigne, the Rollo Suavely of his day, replied: 'I come all this way to be called sex-obsessed?' What good he was to the Alliance was not clear.

A questioner asked the old question: which of the two Davids would become Prime Minister in an Alliance government? It received its reply, Mr Steel acting as the feed and Dr Owen as the straight man, thus:

Mr Steel: 'I think the audience might be biased in this city.'

Dr Owen: 'It would be that person whose party had the greater number of MPs.'

But in spite of this make-believe, and in spite of Mr Gascoigne, the rally succeeded well. Dr Owen and Debbie were surrounded by admirers as they left. He is a hero in his home town, and she is well known from having done the work of six men in the constituency while her husband was away campaigning around the country.

But next morning there was a meeting of candidate, supporters, and the Press, such as most election campaigns come to at one time or another. The *Western Morning News* had given one sentence to Dr Owen's speech on secondary picketing. The previous evening's TV hardly touched it, preferring Steel on Mrs Thatcher. In the morning, in an upstairs room in a pub on the edge of Dartmoor, half the Press didn't turn up. They were still in bed, either dog tired or having dined too well, or both. Informed sources said one reporter had gone up and down in the lift all night. So, the morning after the night before, Press and candidates just went through the motions.

Had the Tweedledum and Tweedledee thing sorted itself out? 'Helped by fog,' said Dr Owen. 'We're getting the right blend of togetherness and apartness.'

There was a lull.

'You're getting sick of churning round country lanes in that coach,' said Owen. 'You're tired.' But then, in the middle of a sentence, he himself suddenly couldn't remember the name of the Foreign Secretary. Wasn't he tired too?

No, he said, but the last bloody election, all he could

afford was a little one-engined thing, and one short hop he
was thrown around so badly he thought he was going to be
sick. When they got down he took a little medicinal brandy,
and then went on this television show. He remembers notic-
ing that the presenter was looking hard at him, having
evidently just asked a question, and realized he had fallen
asleep.

Then there was said to be some new poll in the *Nursing
Times* showing that more than forty per cent of nurses
preferred Alliance policies.

We went ouside. In the deserted yard the security men
waited with their three cars – one red, one white, one blue,
but otherwise inconspicuous. Everyone looked warily at the
Dartmoor skyline where Dr Owen and his wife and children
were due to be photographed feeding ponies. They were.
An animal-lover, having observed this, protested that it was
illegal under some by-law. Just a politician's stunt, she said,
no better than kissing babies.

Dr Owen, to his daughter Lucy: 'Your apples got me into
trouble, mate.'

Lucy: 'It's you who thought of the apples, not me.'

Dr Owen: 'Some bloody protection society. Bloody regu-
lations about everything.'

After lunch, in the bus on the long haul out of Plymouth,
Dr Owen pointed out Plympton, which he said had had
two MPs before Plymouth had any. Sir Joshua Reynolds
was mayor. He pointed out the Plympton sewage works
where at the age of seventeen he worked for Costain as a
labourer in the long vacation and earned his first wages. He
remembered queueing up for his pay packet on a Thursday
and seeing the man in front of him trembling for fear he
might be laid off. Costain were good employers, but in
those days they thought they were generous if they told a
man there'd be another contract and more work for him in
five weeks' time.

We entered deep Devon. The sign-posts said Barton
Surges, and then Honiton. 'Up Ottery, Down Ottery, and
Ottery St Mary,' said Dr Owen, in the authentic accent of

deep Devon. We were in countryside where the railway, which must have been built about 1850, was more modern than the roads, which were at best the remains of the old turnpikes. Some time after three o'clock the road ceased to make any pretence at being more than a lane, then we turned into an even narrower lane, and that gave way to a track. Then, in a drizzle, we came to what looked like a film-set out of *Cold Comfort Farm*. To the left was a rusty and derelict corrugated-iron barn. To the right stood a building which I was to learn had once been a calf shed. In the middle of the yard was a farm trailer on which Dr Owen mounted. And there, amazingly, was a crowd of farmers, and farmers' wives carrying children in their arms. There must have been two hundred of them, gathered in the middle of no-where, believed to be near Sidbury, in the constituency of Honiton. No one could ever have thought the constituency better than hopeless. It is one of the most Conservative in England. Most times since the war the Liberals had finished second, but they were so confident they never had a chance that they gave it to the SDP to fight this time. You could say their candidate, Mr Gerald Tatton-Brown, had a well-sounding name, but that was all he had going for him.

On his farm cart, Dr Owen talked about milk quotas, said he had a great sympathy for the yeomen of England, and then began a lament which sounded like something out of Goldsmith's *Deserted Village*. If the small farmer went to the wall, then the village school would go, and then the creamery, and then the garage, and then there was devastation.

Then, as it happened, came rain – real country-fresh rain. Dr Owen ignored it for a while and then looked up at it. His audience did not budge, not a man, not a woman, not a dog. So he stood his ground and invited questions. 'How do you have the gall,' asked a woman in pearls and welling-ton boots, 'to stand there and ask us to vote Alliance and let Labour in?' The downpour increased. A man in a tweed coat, huddling next to me against a wall, said,

'Aren't many farmers here now anyway. Lot of derelict land.'

An ex-Navy man asked a question showing he preferred to scrap nuclear weapons and preserve the Navy. Dr Owen said we didn't need an all-singing, all-dancing nuclear weapon, but we did need something nuclear, and he would anyway keep a fifty-frigate Navy. He then discussed the rotation of crops.

'But how are we going to pay our farm workers?' asked a clear-voiced woman. The women were all admirable. They could all have run Crown colonies. I have seen and admired their like in Rhodesia when it was still Rhodesia, before Dr Owen, as Foreign Secretary, tried to negotiate it away for them. Dr Owen then talked about the keeping open of country lanes. He said it took only three years for a country lane to grow over completely. I don't know where he got this from, but no one denied the truth of it. 'We've kept the small, winding country roads,' he said. I knew this to be true myself, from that day's travels, but could see no electoral advantage in it, either way. The pelting downpour got worse. I edged along the derelict wall until I found a derelict door which yielded to a push, and took shelter in a derelict building. 'Calf-rearing shed,' said the helpful man in tweeds next to me.

The downpour became a torrent. The farmers and farmers' wives stood their sodden ground. It was such a moment as to make any man – viewing all this from the shelter of a calf-rearing shed, through a smashed window – feel proud to be English. Someone shouted, 'Give the land a chance.' Dr Owen then promised them all a cup of tea in the rusty barn, only they would have to pay for it themselves otherwise it might be construed as illegal treating by the candidate.

We went on, very late, to Taunton, where the meeting was so crowded that the constituency agent who organized it found himself stuck outside, unable to squeeze or even barge his way in. But Taunton was hopeless too, whatever Mr Heath's special information might have been. From there it was going to take an hour and a half to get to Swindon, and Dr Owen wanted to talk. I went to the back of the bus where he and his wife and three children were perched on a bouncing, squashy sort of banquette which ran round the sides. They all hated it, and it was much less comfortable there than in the ordinary seats farther forward, but it was the coach company's idea of luxury.

Dr Owen started off on Mr Kinnock's use of the word 'occupation'. As I saw it, what Mr Kinnock had said on television was that Britain didn't need nuclear weapons because any attempt to occupy western Europe, or certainly Britain, would be utterly untenable, and that any potential enemy knew that very well. His political opponents thereupon pounced on this as a putting of faith in a sort of Home Guard or Mujahedin, Afghan style. Nearly everything's fair in an election. Probably Mr Kinnock wasn't advocating guerrilla war as the only defence against a Russian attack, but even to mention the word 'occupation' was asking for it. Dr Owen said he thought it was a Freudian slip of the tongue.

And after defence, he said, the most emotional issue for him was education. 'Why do we tolerate these strikes? It really tears me up. There's almost an anti-learning culture.'

Among the teachers too? 'Oh, yes.' He said his two sons went to a comprehensive school. Because the teachers refused to attend in the evening, the parent-teacher meeting had to be held in the afternoon, at half-past three. 'I had to decide whether or not to miss Prime Minister's question time. Now, I could say to hell with that, and go to the meeting. A lot of people couldn't. They had to go to work.'

What about those people who were happy to vote for him, but weren't so happy about the Alliance? 'They can't separate the two out. That is what's on offer. It's warts and all.'

What about the Alliance's yellow tie, which he'd worn to launch the party's new colour, but not, I thought, since? He said two ties had been bought, and David Steel had been given the first choice. The second tie was pretty awful. He wore the bloody tie. He'd never worn it since. He would never wear it again.

I had got up and was about to go back to my seat when he told me to sit down again because there was something he wanted to get across. It was plain that everything he had in mind depended on a hung parliament. That wasn't looking likely, and without that there was nothing in it for the Alliance. But even given that, what then?

'Over the next ten days,' he said, 'people have got to realize that what we are determined to achieve is a very tough bargain. There's too much talk of our being an appendage to a Thatcher government or a Kinnock government.'

Yes? 'That is not worth our while. We would have an endorsement of a quarter to one-third of the electorate . . .'

No, that wasn't the way things worked. The Alliance might have, say, forty MPs: put it that way. 'No. The winner-take-all system changes. When you've got twenty MPs (and it was he who changed my suggested figure of forty to twenty), and you've got twenty or thirty per cent of the vote, you are absolutely screwed when they have got a majority. One is enough.'

True, but how did that help him? 'But one is enough the other way too, and if they're dependent on you for building a government they've got to bloody well listen to you. If they don't want to listen . . .'

What then? 'Have a second election.'

Oh, and that would make him popular? 'That is too widely assumed, that it wouldn't be popular. We've insured against a second election. We've got more money for a second election than we have for the first. The Liberal Party has got more money for the second election than for the first. We're going to get a million; they've insured up to a million quid.'

We arrived at Swindon, where he addressed the last meeting of the day. The SDP candidate was dull. Afterwards, back in the bus, someone told Owen: 'You missed a trick there. Swindon were promoted to the second division last night.' The canned beer on the bus ran out. At 9.25 we left the motorway and, again in the middle of nowhere, found Ye Olde Red Lion, where twenty cans of lager were bought, and cider for Debbie. David Owen, who had stayed in the bus, had to stride off towards the Red Lion and exert his authority to get the reporters out of the pub and get going again. 'The time', he told them, 'has come.'

On the way back to London he came and chatted to those who remained, putting his feet up, drinking cider, and foretelling the future of the Labour Party. If it did very badly this time, then Kinnock would go, but not for a while. He would trim to the left, but then, after two years or so, the union would ditch unilateralism, there would be a new leader, and Labour would go right.

Now I was listening to this with half an ear, between transcribing what I had on tape of David Owen saying how hard a bargain he would drive. So I could not be certain of what I heard next. Someone asked, well, if that were so, if Labour did go right, what would happen to the SDP? That is what I thought he was asked. I did not hear it clearly, but it was the whole trend of the conversation, and that is what I understood. What I did hear clearly was Dr Owen's answer. He said one word, and it sounded almost casual. 'Dies,' he said.

Now I could not use this. If a politician comes and talks to reporters on his bus, and doesn't expressly say something is off the record, then it's fair game. But I hadn't clearly heard the question he was asked. Nor could I ask him if he meant what I thought he meant, because he would then have qualified it. It would have been natural self-preservation to do so. So in what I wrote for the *Guardian* the next day, I just reported the parts of conversation I had heard clearly, and added my own question at the end: 'And what of the SDP then?'

I reported what I knew he had wanted me to report about the driving of tough bargains: he had, after all, said it, though we both knew he was just whistling to keep up his party's spirits. But I also wrote what had been quite obvious, that he looked desperately alone, a politician of distinction without a party.

EIGHT

Dr Hammer, Mrs Thatcher, and the Kremlin Lift

We were into the second half of a long election campaign, and a diversion was welcome. It was provided by the visit to London of Dr Armand Hammer, who is a fable. He is going on ninety. He has made fortunes in wheat, asbestos, pencils and oil. He is a man who has travelled on a scheduled airline only once in the last twenty years. For the most part he flies round the world in his own private jet, looking down and getting a broad, international view of things. He is a man who in his long life has known Lenin, Roosevelt, Brezhnev, Gorbachev, Tony Benn, and Mrs Thatcher. So he also takes a longer view of things. I did remind him, as we were talking, that we were in the middle of an election. 'Yes, that's why I don't want to be seen to be trying to promote Mrs Thatcher. It might work against her. I don't know.' [Laughter.]

Well, great events would bring us to Mrs Thatcher in the course of the conversation, but we began with the Kremlin lift. Or rather, before that, there were formalities to be got through. He was staying at Claridges and I went there to meet him. I was received by Sir Ranulph Twistleton-Wykeham-Fiennes, third baronet and polar explorer, who helps Dr Hammer when he is in London. Then we went up to Dr Hammer's two suites. We waited to be let in with a key. Then an American aide, acting with all the convoluted fuss that sometimes passes in big American corporations for efficiency, said that Doctor was not ready yet, that Doctor was running late, that there were urgent letters to be seen by Doctor, and that Doctor was on the telephone, it was thought to China. He was always referred to by this American as Doctor, not Dr Hammer, or the doctor, but Doctor. Sir Ranulph took no notice of all the fuss and chatted to me about the impossibility of understanding what it was like at sixty degrees below.

Then Doctor was free, and we went into a second suite, and he was as easy as you like to get on with. So I began with the Kremlin lift. Yes, the last time he had been there, to see Gorbachev after Chernobyl, he had gone up in the same lift that he had known since the days of Lenin, a little lift like those in Paris apartment houses, with room for only three people.

Armand Hammer is an American whose parents were of Russian extraction. He graduated in medicine at Columbia, and then in 1921 went to Russia where, in the bright revolutionary dawn, famine was flourishing. He found he could be of more use as an importer of American wheat, in exchange for furs and minerals, and this was why he first went up in the Kremlin lift to see Lenin, who very well understood that businessmen were not philanthropists, and gave him trade concessions. He imported the first Fordson tractors into Russia, which were demonstrated to no less a man than the young Mikoyan. For years Dr Hammer controlled all US–Soviet trade.

Now I remembered Michael Caine, who knows Hammer, once telling me a story. Lenin had asked Hammer if the revolution would work. Hammer had thought, and replied no. Lenin had also thought, and then agreed. Was this true? As Dr Hammer remembered it, things were not quite that way. Lenin had told him simply that communism wasn't working, that he had to change to a new economic policy, and that businessmen like Hammer could do things. 'I appreciate Michael's statement, but he really paraphrased it.'

But Dr Hammer was kind to Lenin, wasn't he? Here was a man who fomented the Bolshevik revolution, who overthrew what might have been the perfectly workable Kerensky regime, and who then tormented the modern history of Europe: wasn't that so? Dr Hammer invited me to consider all the crimes committed by the Czars, and the pogroms, and the fact that Lenin's beloved brother had been killed for plotting to kill the Czar. And the serfs, he said, were really slaves.

But surely the serfs had been freed by the Czar in 1860 or so? 'Yes, but before that.'

But Lenin must have killed hundreds of thousands? 'You know, revolution is no game of ping-pong. Revolution is war. How many people get killed in a war? There was no question in my mind that Lenin, when I described to him the scenes I had seen, in the famine areas, his eyes filled with tears. It means there was some good in him. He wasn't Stalin. Stalin was a monster. I avoided him.'

I must have looked unconvinced, because Dr Hammer went on: 'People who are emotional are not all bad. Take Brezhnev for example.' He said Madame Furtseva, describing Brezhnev to him when she was Minister of Culture, had put her hand over her heart. And when he had met Brezhnev to give him two holograph letters of Lenin's, Brezhnev, having no reciprocal gift prepared, impulsively took his own gold watch and chain and gave it to him. 'We're dealing with human beings. They're not all black. They're not all white. Of course, the execution of the Czar and his family was a horrible thing . . .'

Yes, and that too was at Ekaterinburg, where Dr Hammer, three or four years later, first saw the Russian famine? 'Yes, so I think you're right to question that, but I have tried to describe him as I saw him.'

Later he had seen Trotsky? 'Oh, those were the eyes of a fanatic. Oh, God. It was a narrow escape that Trotsky didn't succeed Lenin, although it might have been the end of communism. He would have provoked a war with the West . . . and that would have been the end of that.'

Trotsky had expected that revolution would spread to the United States? 'No doubt about it. He would have spread revolution by force. That's where Gorbachev – I believe we have a break [a chance] with Gorbachev. Gorbachev is perceptive enough to see that capitalism is not going away, as these fellows [his predecessors] have all thought. We have plenty of faults, but we do get things done, and civilization moves ahead. We have a better standard for more people than the Russians have. That's why Gorbachev is trying to make socialism work. I happen to feel he won't succeed, because I don't think that you can make socialism work.'

Well, had it ever been done? 'No,' he said. He had met Kadar, the Hungarian leader, two days before, and they had discussed communism. He had told Kadar he had made it work because he had mixed it with capitalism.

Kadar: 'Not capitalism, but I allow for human nature.'

Hammer: 'What's the difference?'

We had talked about Trotsky's eyes. Dr Hammer compares them with those of Tony Benn, whom he met more than forty years later, when Mr Benn was Energy Secretary and Dr Hammer was getting into North Sea oil. 'He had the same look of a fanatic. Although I liked him and he liked me.'

We began comparing Franklin Roosevelt and Lenin, both of whom Dr Hammer sees as being cut from the same 'extraordinary cloth of humanity' from which he believes leaders are made. Roosevelt was one of his heroes, and so was Winston Churchill.

What did they have in common? Perhaps a certain 'can do'?

'That's it. That's it. And courage.' He remembered the courage of FDR when he was wheeled into Madison Square Garden, held up by his son Jimmy. This was in the depression of the early thirties. Capitalism was falling apart. When he saw this, there were tears in Hammer's eyes for Roosevelt's courage.

Hadn't he called Mrs Thatcher majestical? 'I like Mrs Thatcher. I think she's a woman of courage. And for a *woman* to do the things she does, to show the courage . . .'

How the Labour women's campaign group, proselytizing

in the Midlands and north, would have hated to hear that: for a *woman* to do such things. But I thought it would be useless to try to explain Labour women to Dr Hammer, or him to them. The incomprehension would be complete. So, instead, I asked Dr Hammer what he saw in Mrs Thatcher's eyes. 'I see that she is dedicated to improving the lot of her people . . . and that she will go down in history as a great leader.'

The first was a lot to see from a few glances: the second, whatever you think of her, is likely to be true.

From Mrs Thatcher we went again to Gorbachev. 'I am a great believer that we have a window in Gorbachev now, to see reductions in nuclear armaments.'

Did he trust Gorbachev? 'Yes, certainly I do. I trust him because his instincts are good.'

But surely the whole history of Russia had been one of imperial expansion? To take it only from 1938, there were Estonia, Latvia, Lithuania, and then after the war East Germany, Hungary, Czechoslavakia . . .? 'Stalin,' said Dr Hammer, in explanation of that terrible list. But in the last two years, since Gorbachev took over, there hadn't been a single country taken over, or turned to communism. You couldn't say that about Brezhnev or Krushchev. Gorbachev was the only one, and that should tell you something about the man. He was intelligent, educated, and a pragmatist.

Gorbachev happened to believe, say, that Russia would go broke if she tried to compete with the United States on star wars? 'You put your finger on it. You've got into the things I believe.'

Now, Dr Hammer had said that in the 1960s Britain was politely sinking into post-imperial and post-industrial decline – did he still believe that? 'No, I think Mrs Thatcher makes all the difference. That's why I admire her so much.'

I said I was sure she would be jolly pleased, and we drifted into a chat about diet books, pencils and credit cards.

Dr Hammer said he had once given Brezhnev a copy of *Dr Atkins's Revolutionary Diet Book*, and guessed that was a good pun, though he hadn't looked at it in that way before.

And as to pencils, why, in the mid-1920s there was a famine of pencils in Russia too, and, having got the concession for pencils, he was soon manufacturing a million a week, each stamped with his name. Krushchev, Brezhnev and Chernenko had all told him they learned to write with Hammer pencils, and a box of them was still preserved in Lenin's old study.

I asked about the time, in the early 1970s, when Dr Hammer and the late Lord Thomson were going into North Sea oil, and Thomson said come for lunch, but found when they got into his Rolls Royce that they only had a single pound note between them, so they had to go to somebody's club to eat. Now hadn't either of them, Thomson or Hammer, had a credit card on him? 'I don't think so. I don't have a credit card that's good in the UK. Maybe American Express is good now. I don't think I had it then.' Good Lord. One knows that the very rich don't carry money, but not to carry credit cards either, and not to be sure whether American Express is good in the UK, when it and at least two other cards have been good worldwide since years before that lunch with Thomson, must be the innocence of the mega-rich.

The American aide was back, being efficient. 'Doctor, we need to interrupt . . . Extreme urgency.'

Dr Hammer was in the middle of saying that something got to the heart of where we were going in this world . . .

Aide, with deferential urgency: 'Your call's going through. Senator Baker.'

Dr Hammer answered the telephone: 'Hullo, Howard! How are you?'

Howard Baker, senator for Tennessee 1972-84, and one of President Reagan's closest allies, might I thought have something interesting to overhear, so I hung around, at least to the extent of not bolting for the door, but the aide had other ideas.

'We'll come back' – this addressed to me with extreme urgency – and I was shepherded into another suite, again. More pressing negotiations were entered into because by

that time Doctor was running *very* late and a photographer
had arrived from the *Financial Times*, for whom arrange-
ments were being made that were amazing in their com-
plexity. Then we were ushered back and Dr Hammer was
informed of the photographic protocol agreed, which was
that he was to move, if he would, to the other side of the
sofa where the light was better.

'A pleasure,' he said.

Fuss, fuss, went the aide.

I made small talk. 'You brought me luck,' said Dr
Hammer. 'The best thing that happened to me.' He was
referring to the telephone call.

Then I asked him about Kipling's poem 'If' – those splendid lines of stiff-upper-lip advice to British imperial man,
circa 1890 – which are said to be an inspiration to him.
'Hangs up in my bedroom,' he said. On his wall he also had
Lincoln saying that he always tried his best but that if
things went wrong ten angels swearing on a stack of Bibles
wouldn't help him, but if things turned out right everything
that had been said against him would be forgotten. He also
had an autograph letter of Einstein's saying that Man only
started to live when he lived outside of himself.

Which were his favourite bits of 'If'?

'Oh . . .'

So I prompted him, reciting:

> If you can meet with Triumph and Disaster
> And treat those two imposters just the same.

'Yes,' he said. 'If you can walk with kings and not lose
the common touch . . . That's great.'

We parted, Dr Hammer inviting me to drop in and see
him when I was in Los Angeles. As I had noticed on his
London programme, which Sir Ranulph had shown me
earlier, he was due to meet the Prince of Wales next morning.

NINE

The Struggle, and God's Sweetest Talker

Five miles north-west of Claridges, in an old shop in Willesden High Road, were the committee rooms of Mr Ken Livingstone. He is the man Mr Kinnock calls a tassel, and loses his temper over. He has the mildest eyes you ever saw. Dr Hammer would be surprised.

Brent East is a constituency where immigrants have traditionally settled. That accounts for the Irish accents in the streets. It accounts for the large detached, prosperous, thirties houses in the southern part of the division, where many Jews live, near the new stadium where the world hockey championships were played in 1986. It accounts for the thirty per cent of the electorate who are black or Asian.

It is a constituency of contrasts. The bad bits are very bad. Think of Kilburn, Neasden, Willesden, and you have it. The last two districts are, as it happens, mostly within the constituency boundaries. It is typical north-west London. But the candidate is evidently a south Londoner. Ken Livingstone was born and raised in south London. His father was a seaman but was working at the Streatham Empire as a scene shifter when he met an acrobatic dancer who was doing the rounds of the halls with Donald Peers. They married. The young Ken Livingstone was fascinated by politics at the age of eleven, while he was still at comprehensive school. He was nineteen when Harold Wilson became

Prime Minister in 1964. He trembled with excitement because he believed that a Labour government would eliminate poverty. He watched as it did not. He now says that he will never again tremble with such expectation, whatever government should be returned. He is to that extent, and only to that extent, a cynic. For the rest, he is another one of Labour's Utopians. He tried to run the Greater London Council as if it were a model settlement of the optimistic nineteenth century, like New Lanark or New Harmony – and look what happened to those, and to the GLC. The first time I ever asked him, some years ago, if he wanted to be an MP, he surprised me with the manner of his answer, which came, and was spoken, in a religious form of words. 'I do.' He said he would then work with Mr Benn and Mr Scargill to change the Labour Party into a force worthy of government.

He wasn't in his committee rooms when I went looking for him, but next door in Ken's restaurant. That Ken is no relation. During the campaign he ate there, and they let him use the washroom, because his own place didn't have one. We started with pleasantries about Mr Kinnock's having lost his cool. 'The Left,' said the amiable Mr Livingstone, who had just been caricatured in the *Daily Express* as a shark devouring a Kinnock-fish, 'is never a threat to anyone. Most of us have trouble getting out of bed in time for a demonstration, let alone being violent.'

What about Russia in 1917, then? 'But they had Lenin. I don't see a British Lenin on the scene at the moment.' Lenin was hyperbole, a Hammer kind of hyperbole, but in the afternoon and evening we spent together Mr Livingstone did manage to cite Edmund Burke, Gladstone, Franklin Delano Roosevelt and Robert F. Kennedy.

He was amused by talk of a left-wing takeover of the Labour Party, though at the same time he wasn't really taking Mr Kinnock too seriously. He saw Kinnock as in a minority on the soft left of the party, the majority being from what he called the right and centre. He took from his pocket a handwritten digest of two newspaper surveys to demonstrate this. Furthermore, he said, in the seats Labour needed to beat the Tories there were more soft Left candidates, and in any case, given the way the party was organized, it wouldn't matter whether Mr Kinnock in government had the support of the majority of his MPs or not, since the Cabinet would run the whole show.

But what he seemed most confident of was a hung parliament. 'We only need that,' he said, 'and we win.' Everyone would then combine to defeat Mrs Thatcher. Could I imagine even the Ulster Unionists voting for her, since they wanted to hang her for the Irish pact? As for the Alliance, Owen's views wouldn't then matter one way or the other: if you were Simon Hughes or Cyril Smith, with large blocks of Labour voters breathing down your neck, were you going to prop up Mrs Thatcher? Then the Queen would send for Neil. Mr Livingstone said he had always thought the way back would be through a minority government. Labour had never won power directly from opposition. Twice in the 1920s, and in 1964, and in February 1974, they'd formed minority governments. Even in 1945 they had won not from opposition but after the wartime coalition.

And perhaps, he said, at this stage it wasn't possible for a radical, urbanized leadership to bring the party to victory, because they would offend traditional working-class voters. The last politician who could deliver the blacks, the poor, and the skilled workers had been Robert Kennedy. He had been able to pick up white racists as well as ninety-eight per cent of the black vote, but after he was assassinated in 1968 the whites went to Nixon the Republican. To that I said that any comparison with the old Democratic Party wouldn't wash. Take its weird traditional coalition of southern bigots, big city Irish, and East Coast liberals. There was nothing like that in British politics. He replied that the Jews and every immigrant group who had come to England had first voted Labour, until it produced its wealthy middle class. As for the intelligentsia, when the old Liberal Party collapsed they all bloody jumped to Labour overnight.

He placed himself firmly on the left? 'I clearly identify myself with Benn, Skinner, Bernie Grant and all that. [But] where you place yourself in the spectrum is one thing. The second question is, do you see that as the Labour Party? I never did. You've got to have a much firmer consensus to do the things you want. There'll never be in my lifetime a Labour Party composed of people that broadly share my political perspective. It's not conceivable.'

Was he a parliamentary democrat? 'Yes. I'm not going to say I'm a House of Commons man. Parliament is the will of the people to achieve change. It's not some sort of club that one joins, and then is divorced from the people that put you there.'

Mr Livingstone is a man whose love of reptiles is famous. He will tell you there are 2,800 species of frog and toad alone, and express surprise that reptiles don't attract the same attention as primates or herd animals. He once did try to get a job at London zoo, but they told him they only took people on in March, and it wasn't March. I reminded him that his Conservative opponent in Brent, who was a woman, had called him a charming snake. 'Ah! I've called myself that before. I've said the fascination some people have with me is the same as when people wander round the reptile house at the zoo. They're engrossed; they think it's beautiful, but they don't want to touch. Fortunately, here they like the reptiles.'

We came to Mr Steel's list of 101 Damnations, Labour MPs of the far left. Mr Livingstone didn't mind at all. He just hoped he wasn't being outflanked on the left, certainly not on lesbian or gay rights, or on Ireland.

Look, lesbian and gay rights: didn't this talk cost him votes?

'Yes.'

Well, wasn't he worried? He said of course he was, but then asked how I could venerate Burke (about whom I had incidentally said nothing) and then complain that he,

Livingstone, was saying what he believed even though it might cost him votes?

What about Mr Kinnock's famous party political broadcast? Had he liked that? 'You remember all the silly things I did at County Hall, and you ask me if I have qualms about that? It worked. What the GLC did was not to put up the slogans we would have liked, but the ones the pollsters told us would win, and we were very happy.'

So if it worked it was all right with him? 'Yes.'

What Mr Livingstone does have, and there is no getting away from it, is a candour which often allows him to give a straight answer. So I asked him how he saw his future. Look, he said, if I had asked him that same question ten years before, he would have said he would win Hampstead in the general election of 1978, and he would have got even the date of the election wrong. It came in 1979 and he lost. If he had won, he would today be an unknown backbench MP. But he lost. Then came the GLC and notoriety. You just couldn't predict. Anything could happen. Nothing could happen.

And what did he think would happen if Labour won the election? Resistance, he thought, by the Civil Service and mendacious judges, and obstruction by Reagan and the Common Market. And the Press would go berserk. Some fanatical right-wingers really believed they'd be forced to attend lesbian classes and that Russians would be in the streets by the end of the year.

At this point one of the family running the café came up to the table with her children and asked what was going to be done about the park just across the road. They talked about it. He said he would see what the council could be asked to do. Then he turned back to me. 'Gladstone Park,' he said. 'I'm going to be MP for Gladstone.' The great man had lived there, on a four-hundred-acre estate, in the years of his last administration.

Good for Livingstone. His connection with Gladstone will be at least as close as Mr Steel's. But we had been talking about backlashes. What did he foresee? Putches? 'Violent anger,' he said.

Well, now suppose Mrs Thatcher won. What about the Labour Party then? He foresaw a substantial swing to the right in the unions, a loss of confidence in the left-wing constituency parties, and conference moving several notches to the right.

Not to the left? To the right?

'I bet you £100 I'm right on this. I don't have one per cent of doubt.'

There, within a few days of each other, were Mr Livingstone and Dr Owen expressing similar views about the future course of a defeated Labour Party. It was a course that would work against both of them. Both knew that. And both look as shrewd men as you could find.

We chatted briefly about socialist matters, and I told him he was a Utopian. He'd heard that before. 'I believe,' he said, 'in the fundamental goodness of humanity. Sorry about that.'

We went in search of some of this goodness, first of all at Willesden bus garage. On the way Mr Livingstone was stopped on the pavement by a young black man who told him: 'I hear you loud and clear. People like you will go places.'

The busmen in their canteen were not so sure. The management didn't want him around, and took him into an office to negotiate terms. They might reasonably have suspected him of subversion, since he was running on a promise to abolish the London Transport Executive, but all they required was an undertaking from him that he would not be accompanied by television cameras. There were mutters from the busmen, who had little confidence in their managers. 'Bloody management,' they said. Mr Livingstone emerged with permission to canvass, saying jauntily, 'I've come to stir up trouble.' The busmen then showed their confidence in him.

'Lesbians and homosexuals,' said one man. 'Spend our money on them? That's no way.'

Mr Livingstone replied that one in ten people who committed suicide did so because they were lesbian or gay. This was the first time I'd ever seen him make a bad political error: they obviously thought this proportion not nearly high enough.

'Gays,' said another. 'And you're going to encourage it?'

'People,' said Mr Livingstone, 'are what they are.' He then slipped in a mention of the needs of the blacks who made up so many of his constituents.

This did not help either.

'Start helping our people, mate. This is our fucking country, not theirs.'

Mr Livingstone gave a reasoned answer to this observation.

'You're the sweetest talker,' said his interlocutor, 'that God ever put breath into.'

Others made their contributions:

'In my lifetime your party has had a go at it four times, and made a fuck-up each time.'

'You should sort out all the queers.'

'Yeah. As soon as two blokes hold hands – give 'em a subsidy.' [Laughter.]

Mr Livingstone is a brave man. In response to an urgent invitation to express disapproval of AIDS, he explained that it was not a homosexual disease. The busmen listened in scornful disbelief, and then changed tack. 'Anybody votes for you, he wants his bleeding brains tested. You get in, in five years' time this country will be broke. Where can you get money from but from the workers?'

Mr Livingstone said Labour would not increase taxes on ordinary people.

'You've got to, mate. Anyway, what would you do in this country without the rich?'

'*You* create wealth,' said Mr Livingstone, 'not the rich.'

This was considered comical by his audience, who had not read their Marx. In spite of all his services to London Transport, London buses were not solid for Livingstone.

As he had himself predicted, his radical urbanized leadership offended the traditional working-class vote. Most of the barracking was from three men, with one eloquent man in the lead, the one who had recognized Mr Livingstone's own qualities as a sweet talker. Not one man in the canteen spoke up for Mr Livingstone. The best he got was this: 'I'll vote for you, mate, but I don't think you've got a chance.' It wasn't encouraging. A man of less equable charm might have been slung out.

Out into the street we went, where another young black man asked him: 'Are you Neil Kinnock? If I get to Mrs Thatcher I'll string her up myself.' Upon which Mr Livingstone remarked that this was probably the most religious constituency in the country – devout Hindus, devout Muslims, devout Roman Catholics, devout Caribbean chapel people. And they'd got him, he said, an agnostic, for their candidate.

Back at his committee rooms he showed me a cutting from the *Irish Post* on the wall. This is a paper read by the Irish in England. He said it had given him the most ringing endorsement he'd ever had. I read the cutting. It said Mr Livingstone had stood with Ireland as no English politician had ever done. Whatever you think of Mr Livingstone, you have to admit he is fearless in collecting political liabilities. On another wall a banner proclaimed 'Strength in Sisterhood'.

His woman agent told him the chair for that night's meeting had cried off. He wasn't alarmed and suggested someone else, of whom his agent had a low opinion. He said it would be all right. 'You say it's a doddle,' she said, 'until the bloody SWP (Socialist Workers' Party) gets up, and then he can't control it.'

The next canvass was at a Guinness brewery. It was too far to walk. He doesn't drive, so he got a beaten-up car from the minicab firm next door. On the way he mentioned that he was not only agnostic but also at heart an anarchist, though he had, he said, somehow managed to square that with the Labour Party organization. Then he talked about a mystical novel called *The Mists of Avalon*. He said it was about the new religion of Christianity driving out the old religion of the druids. The story of the snakes being driven out of Ireland by St Patrick was really that of the druids being driven out, because there had never been snakes in Ireland. He said Arthur had been a most powerful legend, but there was no mention of him in the Venerable Bede's *Ecclesiastical History of England*.

If that had been said by plenty of other Labour men I could think of, it would have been suggesting a Bedeian conspiracy of suppression. Mr Livingstone didn't mean that, but he was, I think, assuming that Bede wasn't going to give unnecessary publicity to the old enemy. He then said witch hunts had survived into the middle ages: that was another remnant of the old religion.

He really does believe in the occult. He said a cousin of his had died three years before. An aunt had a premonition of this before she could have known of the death. I asked him how he explained this. He said that there was great energy in a living creature. If all this energy was somehow discharged at the moment of death, perhaps it would have the power to communicate the news of its own death.

We got to Guinness, where the meeting was in a clubroom overlooking acres of green space and a bowling green. The shop stewards he addressed here were more amenable than the busmen, but were probably readers of the capitalist Press against which he immediately warned them. 'Unless you actually hear a Labour politician saying it,' he said, 'don't believe a thing.' He talked about the chance of a nuclear-free zone in Europe, and about the way the Thatcher government had deliberately kept unemployment up to undermine the power of the trade unions. The shop stewards were more concerned about the high rates imposed by the local Labour councils and about Mr Livingstone's Irish policy: how were they going to explain that to the men on the shop floor? It was just as well they had not seen the cutting from the *Irish Post* pinned on his wall.

Mr Livingstone's presentation of himself was masterly. First he took off his sports coat and loosened his tie: that was for approachability. But then, when he was asked a question, he always rose to his feet to give the answer: that's for courtesy. He wasn't taught this at any socialist weekend school, not even at the Red Chinese course in subversion which he likes to kid people he attended as soon as he left school. It comes naturally to him, and he is the more dangerous for this. He is the sort of man whom people follow. Men like him set fashions, which afterwards become recognized as the rules of the game.

'What about apprenticeships?' one man asked him. Why was it only those who were well educated, those who had four or five O-levels, who had a chance? It's at times like this that it comes home to an observer just how low some British standards have become. Here was a man in whose world a boy or girl would be well educated with four or five O-levels. Mr Livingstone answered, saying it was true there were ten apprenticeships in Germany for every one here, and that in the United States three times as many went to university as did here. Then he went off at one of his unpredictable tangents and praised Cuban schools, of which he knows little and of which his audience very likely knew nothing. But you could see, and it was astonishing that so sensitive a politician as Mr Livingstone did not also see, that the shop stewards didn't like his mention of Cuba one bit.

One of the shop stewards gave him a lift back. As we passed a hoarding advertising non-alcoholic lager, Mr Livingstone, whose drink is white wine, looked forward to the day when someone would devise a non-alcoholic Chablis. We passed many Asians in the streets. He said there were now thirty-five Patel millionaires in the country, and that two or three lived in his constituency. The Jews had tended recently to move further out of London, to Harrow. The Irish had been here since the early nineteenth century. In the last three years they had poured in. A Catholic priest he knew had told him more were coming into Brent now than

at any time since the famine of the 1840s. We passed the
North Circular Road, which is one of the boundaries of
Brent East, and Mr Livingstone, seeing a signpost to
Neasden, said that he would be MP not only for Gladstone
but also for Neasden: he hoped that would please *Private
Eye*.

We got back to his committee rooms, and arranged to
meet at a school where he had a rally that evening. He smiled
at the word rally, and said I would see for myself. To kill
time I wandered into one of Brent council's public libraries.
A poster advertised 'Marxism 87', a week of forthcoming
debates.

The rally was in a school gym. At the door was a framed
drawing of an Indian child saying Welcome in two
languages. I could not recognize the first language. The
second was English. The picture was surrounded by a rubric
of words in Bengali, Arabic, Punjabi, Yoruba, Urdu and
Gaelic. The Gaelic said Failte, so I supposed the different
languages were all saying Welcome again. I don't know
what call there can have been for Yoruba. Outside, two
people tried to sell the communist *Morning Star*. I saw no
takers. Inside, eighty-four people gathered.

Mr Livingstone took off his coat again. He warned his
audience against fake handouts, purporting to be his, in
which he was said to be in favour of arming shop stewards
to defend their factories, and in favour of dropping nuclear
bombs on America. Again he told them, 'Believe nothing
about me unless you hear it from my lips.' He said that the
week before he had been followed by fifteen reporters in
taxis, all hoping to observe something that they could dis-
tort. Speaking in front of a frieze of children's drawings of
the transport of the future, he said he wanted to lift the
burden of poverty from the Third World. He said that since
1945 only Argentina had declined in manufacturing power
as rapidly as Britain. And we had fought Argentina. 'Like
we had to squabble to see who's bottom of the pile at the
end of the day.'

As for the House of Commons, he expected that when

he got there he would find it much as he found County Hall when he arrived – a Stalinist mausoleum. Then, once again, his spots of political blindness came upon him, as he said, 'We let in the gays, the lesbians, the animal rights groups, and gave them rooms. That building came to life. We reached out and touched people.' This was an audience composed almost entirely of his supporters, but there was still no wild enthusiasm at the mention of these fringe causes. And Mr Livingstone must know what wins votes and what loses them. His election leaflet, the one that went through every letter box in the constituency, the one the Post Office delivered free for him, naturally made a great deal of his time as Leader of the GLC. That is his principal fame. But in that pamphlet there is no mention of the Irish, or gays or lesbians. But as soon as he got on his feet, he couldn't stop himself.

Then a man called out: 'Why are you here tonight? You hijacked Reg Freeson.'

Several voices: 'Shut up.'

Livingstone: 'No, don't shut him up. If he feels like that, he's done well to keep quiet for the last half an hour.'

The Freeson story was bound to come up somehow. Reg Freeson was educated in a Jewish orphanage in West Norwood, was a Willesden councillor by 1952 and chairman of Brent council by 1964, and became an MP the same year. He was Minister for Housing in the Wilson and Callaghan governments. But he fell out with his increasingly left-wing constituency party, kept the nomination by the skin of his teeth in 1983, and this time was ousted to make room for Livingstone.

For the moment, though, that topic was allowed to drop. Mr Livingstone talked about pensioners. They knew, he said. They knew what could be done. They knew because in 1945 they had elected a government which had turned the world on its head. They knew it could be done again. Then he went on to his demand for a New Deal. In the United States in 1932, he said, the Americans elected a new President. On the day he took office, the banks were closing, and people were riddled with fear. That President was Franklin Delano Roosevelt. He gave the name in full. Pensioners there might still remember his first speech to the American nation. He told them they had nothing to fear but fear itself. But now in Britain we had seen our own government use fear as a weapon against its own people.

Then the Freeson supporters came back at him. 'I've lived in Brent since 1951,' said a man. 'Reg Freeson came out of an orphanage and did a lot for Brent. You hijacked him. Why should I vote for you? You're talking around the bush, around the trees. You're going to be MP for here, not Russia. Why should I vote for you?'

Mr Livingstone explained. If he hadn't been adopted for Brent East someone else would have been, and it wouldn't have been Reg Freeson. (This was true as far as it went, but Livingstone had single-mindedly set about getting the nomination.) Now, he said, the relationship between a constituency party and the MP was like a marriage. The marriage between Reg Freeson and the party had broken down. It had fallen apart. That was the way it was.

Up to a point, that was so. There was no more barracking on the Freeson issue. Livingstone was accepted as the people's candidate. That may cause him trouble yet. At the bottom of his election address, Ken Livingstone said of himself, in red letters: 'The record shows he has been prepared to oppose the party when it has not been working in the best interests of ordinary working-class families, and he intends to continue that struggle.' By 'the party' there he meant the party nationally. He knows where the party places him in the spectrum. He will champion the working class of Brent, and continue its struggle.

The struggle won't be difficult to find in Brent. The shabby ads in shabby newsagents' windows tell the story. There aren't many council estates there, except in the slums in the south of the constituency. The slums in the north are private. A third of the accommodation there is still privately rented, which means, for the most part, grotty bedsits. The ads in the windows are on postcards. They are written out in capital letters and a semi-literate script. The tale they tell is one of poverty:

DOUBLE ROOM TO LET
Cooking facilities
Working people only

FAST CASH LOANS: £30 – £300

ONE SINGLE ROOM TO LET
Working person proffer
Thank you

TEN

Second City, Comrades, and Friends

Birmingham is England's second city, and of all English big cities the most hideously defaced by the improvements of the sixties and seventies. It is also the capital of the west Midlands, a region which, though still prosperous, has a vivid sense of grievance and betrayal, because it is not what it was. As I heard the president of the engineering workers put it, 'I grew up in it and saw its power. Some malice that we can't understand has pulled it down.' Nowhere else do you hear such vilification of the Japanese and Germans for making motor cars that go, and that people buy. There is thought to be some malice in this too.

The collapse of the British car industry is a dismal story of incompetent management and bloody-minded workers, but it is not a matter for this book. I have heard Tony Benn say with bewildered anger, nearly in tears of anger, that he has seen the motor industry destroyed and the motorbike industry destroyed. He blamed Mrs Thatcher's government. I don't, but I know how he feels and I have some idea what the president of the engineering union meant, because I do by chance know Birmingham and the Midlands a bit. I shall explain how.

When I was a very small boy my father's work as an engineer took him over large parts of England, particularly to the Midlands. The company for which he worked, on the south coast, made huge presses the size of a house. I

never knew exactly what they did, but I knew they could
stamp out pieces of metal, anything from eyelets to panels
for cars. My father and a small group of men would install
one of these presses in a factory in, say, Birmingham,
Coventry, or Wolverhampton. My father would then stay
with the press for six months, I suppose to see that it worked
and to run it in. He would take my mother and my brother
and me with him. That is why I went to fourteen schools
in all, and to twelve of those in my first six years of
schooling. That way I got to know the Midlands – the Bull
Ring at Birmingham, where my mother bought a Christmas
chicken for one and sixpence, when chicken was not as
ordinary as it has become; Dudley zoo, which was a day's
outing; and the Coventry Road, running out of Birmingham, where we rented a house whose number was, to my
amazement, one thousand and something. Roads were not
so long down south.

Then my father went into business on his own account,
and went broke because his customers were themselves
broke and unable to pay him. We had to get back to
Bournemouth, where we could stay at my grandmother's.
I have a vivid recollection of how we did this. It is an exact
recollection, though I have no idea whether it is accurate.
My father had the sum of seven pounds ten shillings. He
had the choice of buying an old car for that amount, and
driving us back, or he could spend the money on the train
fare. He doubted whether the car would get that far without
breaking down. We had no money to pay for lodgings if
we did break down on the way. So we came back by train.
It was mid-winter and there was snow on the ground. I
remember it as a trans-Siberian journey. I clearly remember
two sets of tracks, in a snowy landscape, crossing each other
on the same level and at right angles. I can still see it. That
is how exact and how inaccurate memory can be. When we
eventually reached Bournemouth West I enquired where our
taxi was. My father pointed to a yellow Bournemouth
Corporation trolley bus.

As for motor cars, my youth was full of them. After

we returned to the south, my father owned three Flying Standards, one after the other, all very much second hand. They were all made in Coventry. The badge on the bonnet used to say, 'Standard, Coventry'. And I had an uncle who dealt in a small way in second-hand cars. His backyard was full of them. There I learned to recognize Austin, Morris, Wolseley, Humber, Hillman, Sunbeam-Talbot, SS, Triumph. We once had a 1928 fourteen-horsepower Hillman, a vast underpowered limousine that had belonged to the Bowes-Lyon family. It broke down on its first trip and had to be sold on. I could have named thirty British makes, and was familiar with the shape of them all. We talked cars. My father said that if he was ever knocked down he hoped it would be by an Armstrong Siddeley. That was a well-engineered motor car. My uncle tried to specialize in Rileys. They all had wooden frames and canvas-covered roofs, and transmissions that gave a distinctive howl that I should instantly recognize if I heard it again today. My uncle was really a plumber by trade, and he never made a go of the cars, but he did teach me how to appraise one. He used to take me with him when he went out buying. His method was to open all four doors, and then give the side of the car a gentle push with his palm. Any wooden framed car with four doors open would rock ominously. He would shake his head, and say nothing. Then he would walk round the car, kicking each of the tyres in turn, always remarking, audibly but as if to himself, 'Bad boots.' I used to walk round the car with him, and nod when he said 'Bad boots.' This walking round a strange car is a habit I have to this day. It has saved me from several dangerously bald tyres on cars which famous car rental firms round the world were idly trying to pass off on me.

Those childhood memories of the Midlands and of motor cars remain with me, strongly enough to make me regret the death of so many makes with lovely names. I am not so angry as Mr Benn, but I am angry that it is now hardly possible to buy a reliable English car unless it is a Rolls Royce or a Jaguar. I drive a German car. I wish it were not

German, but no English car would make sense. My wife has an English car and when it comes back sloppily serviced, and with half the work undone, as it generally does, I do feel regret and anger. Sir Michael Edwardes once told me that when he went to run British Leyland, as it then was, some of the factories were out of control, that the Japanese could eat BL for breakfast, that only twenty per cent of the whole shooting match was saleable, and that the quality of the bulk of the cars was unacceptable. I then asked him about a previous car of my acquaintance, one of his shooting match, and he said first that he was not a line manager, and then that, having by then left BL, he couldn't go into a product discussion.

There was still a week of campaigning to go when I travelled up to Birmingham by train. The car I picked up from Godfrey Davis at New Street station when I arrived was not the model I had asked for and which they had agreed to supply. This can happen anywhere, but the American routine is to offer first apologies, and then a car one size up, anything to keep the customer happy. At Godfrey Davis, no explanation was offered, or anything else. I drove out to meet Denis Healey at a school in Edgbaston where he was taking part in a mock election.

Now Mr Healey is a card. Mr Kinnock had made himself recognizable during the election. After him, Mr Healey was easily the best-known Labour man. The rest were nowhere. At Harborne Hill school, in the headmaster's office, Mr Healey was doing his actor–manager turn.

He was told the Conservative speaker would be so and so, and the Alliance man so and so. He nodded with that famous gravity. 'I'll give you an impartial speech,' he boomed, laughed heartily when this was for a moment taken seriously, and then went on to say, in response to a question from one of the masters, that, though he would not quite qualify to be Father of the House in the next parliament, he would be Godfather.

It was an unusual school, pleasantly old fashioned in tone. It was opened in 1952 as a state co-educational secondary

school, has six hundred pupils, and still has rules. Pupils are
expected to wear uniform and walk on the left in the corri-
dors, and homework is compulsory. Noise should also be
kept to a minimum. Mr Healey soon did for that last rule,
gathering the children round him on the way from the
headmaster's study to the hall, and demanding to know who
was voting Labour. They told him. 'Louder,' he demanded.
'I can't hear.' And so on.

He then mounted the platform and began to explain
Labour policies. 'We want', he said, 'a society in which
people who are too old to work are looked after. [Pause.]
Some people say I am too old to work.' [Laughter.]

He gave them a regulation dose of party cant. The Government had declared war against teachers and even on head
teachers. South Africa was bad for you. That sort of thing.
But no man of such vigorous intellect can go on for long
without breaking into sense. So, after a bit, he suddenly
said: 'Economics is a pseudo-science, which I advise you to
be wary about.' The pupils, who were a bright lot, quite
liked being told this by an ex-Chancellor of the Exchequer.
Then, reminding them that Mrs Thatcher was due to go to
the economic summit at Venice the following week, he said
she would be photographed in a gondola and nothing would
be done. An ex-Chancellor would know that too.

Then he answered questions, telling Charlie Williams, a
black boy, that he, Healey, had a friend of the same name
who was one of the best comics in the world. Football
hooligans? Well, Britain's reputation there depended not so
much on who was Prime Minister as on what the fans did
when they went abroad. When could you get a council
house? 'Only when there's a Labour government.' This
sounds like something out of a Christmas cracker, but it
was good stuff the way he put it over. He explained about
'a local tax called the rates'. He was enjoying himself, and
the children lapped it up. The headmaster, Mr C. J. James,
then told a story. He had once taken his daughter to see 10
Downing Street. As they got near the house, the door of
No. 11 opened and Mr Healey appeared. An American

tourist went up to him and said she just had to tell her friends that she had shaken the great man's hand. 'You were gracious and gentlemanly,' the headmaster told Mr Healey. 'And you spoke to them for several minutes and I thought, "There's a gentleman".'

No, there was a politician. But the children went hurrah, and Mr Healey then told them a story of his own. A girl of eighteen had accosted him in a railway carriage. [Pause.] And she told him she had danced for him in Downing Street. [Pause.] Years before, when she was eight. And she said she had since made a career as a dancer and was in the chorus of *Starlight Express*. [Applause.]

And so, having delighted them not too long but just long enough, the Gromyko of the Labour Party, alias the Donald Wolfit of the Labour Party, went on his way. He was not, alas, going to the rally at Brierley Hill that evening.

Brierley Hill, fifteen miles west of Birmingham, is a small industrial town which used to be a constituency on its own but is now just the Labour part of what has been, since 1979, the increasingly Conservative seat of Dudley West. The borough of Dudley is active in the Arts. It had recently put on *Hamlet* – 'a play about human nature at its worst and its best' – in Halesowen nearby. The 'Versewagon' with Channel 4 poet Ian McMillan, had visited Dudley, tickets £1.75 to include a glass of wine. The Hallé had played in Dudley Town Hall, where Richard Baker had also presented 'A Baker's Dozen' of his favourite melodies. And *South Pacific* had been staged at the Brierley Hill Civic Hall, where the Labour rally was held that night.

The principal speaker was Mr John Smith, a Scottish lawyer who was Trade Secretary in Mr Callaghan's government, and one of the recommenders of Neil Kinnock in the celebrated TV commercial. Mr Smith is a man who is not one of nature's rabble rousers, but he did say that Thatcher and Tebbit had been the joint wreckers of manufacturing industry in the west Midlands. He was also due to say, according to the speech handed out beforehand, that the once great powerhouse of British industry had been brought almost to a standstill. He added a little zest to this by saying instead that the powerhouse had been brought to its knees. If British industry were a motor car, he said, Lord Young would be tampering with the speedometer and Nigel Lawson would be respraying the bodywork. Let him say unequivocally, he said, that under Labour the Austin Rover group would stay British and stay public.

Which to me – who had just driven a heavy, clumsy, and generally ordinary Montego out of Birmingham in heavy traffic – was a matter of indifference. After all, the best of the Rover group's cars are in large part Hondas, and I only wished the Montego was one of them. But it was no matter of indifference to the audience. They were not responsible for designing mediocre cars, and could hardly be asked to see that it was such mediocrity that had helped to lose them their comfortable and profitable jobs.

Mr Smith said there had to be an industrial renaissance. He had a regulation hack at people making money in the City of London, and at investment in Taiwan or South Africa. He then had a second crack at financiers, and was loudly applauded. He said we ought to have the best educated workforce in western Europe, and by workforce he meant everyone from MP down. The German worker produced twice as much as the English worker and was paid twice as much. And why was this? Because he had twice the technological power at his elbow. Ninety-four per cent of the jobs lost since 1979 had been lost north of a line drawn from the Severn to the Wash.

He then said that Mrs Thatcher had expected to walk this election. But you could tell from the press, from the poll due to be revealed on a television programme that evening, and from the falling prices on the Stock Exchange, that things were not turning out like that. [Loud applause.]

'I've never seen such a strong, echoing response,' he said. [Cheers.]

There was an echo. I had counted 189 people in a hall which could hold 600. The balcony was roped off, the people up there having been induced to come down to fill the front seats.

The chairman then rose. He was famous. His name was Tony Robinson and he appeared in a television show called 'Black Adder'. You could not say he really acted as chairman. He stood at one side, and then performed a routine into a microphone. He had picked up a copy of the *Sun*. 'I know,' he said, 'I should have worn a condom or surgical gloves.' There was a story which said BEASTIE BOY TO STAND TRIAL. He thought it was about Norman Tebbit. Then on page three there was a girl with a blue rosette on her breast. Her boyfriend was a Conservative candidate. It was difficult to tell which was the biggest tit.

When the laughter subsided, he did his serious bit. When the election had begun he had taken a deep breath and got ready for a long slog. But now it was an adventure, and they were confident. The leadership was strong. It was great to see John [Smith] speaking as he had that evening. He had looked at the list of left-wingers which the Alliance had produced – Diane Abbott, Ken Livingstone, Tam Dalyell. All he saw there were capable, talented administrators. Labour was especially strong on defence. Only Labour had a mature understanding of defence, defence without 'murder weapons' like nuclear bombs.

Then up rose Ms Christine Crawley, a tutor in social skills, one of Birmingham's members of the European Parliament, and a member also of the Labour women's campaign which had held baby Amy aloft more than two weeks before.

'Comrades,' she cried, and declared that the word she had found most often in the Tory manifesto was Falklands. (This must have been her unique experience.) She had looked in vain for words like care, jobs, youth. She dismissed the Alliance as a canary-coloured conundrum. She said that to the Tories an electorate in need was a bloody nuisance. She excoriated multi-national corporations and newspaper proprietors, and commended the inhabitants of a battered women's refuge in Wales.

Then she entered the more thoughtful part of her address.

'Let us devastate pain – the real enemy within.' Let them, she said, have their own national health deterrent. The next Labour government would press the button on pain, and it would lose *Her* the election.

The word *Her*, spoken with the right contemptuous emphasis, means only one thing in the world of Ms Crawley.

It was *Her* who had said it was *Her* right to pay to have medical treatment . . . [Cries of 'Shame.']

To have the doctor of *Her* choice when *She* wanted him. ['Shame.']

'What do we want, comrades? We want *Her* OUT.' [General yells.]

The next speaker was on his feet.

'Friends,' he began. That is a form of address likely but not certain to indicate that he is on the left of the party. There are subtleties in Labour Party forms of address. 'Comrade,' used in private, as when shaking hands in a pub, is a sign of leftness, but used in the plural, when addressing a meeting, is neutral. Unless, that is, it is spoken with violence, in which case the speaker will be of the caring, pacifist far left. To begin with 'Friends' is equally ambiguous. It started on the left, but can now be used by someone not of the left who wishes not to offend an audience which may be distinctly left. The Labour Party is full of rifts into which an unwary man may fall. This breeds wariness. The subtlety of English forms of address has always puzzled strangers, and Labourspeak is one of the subtlest of all codes. What is not subtle is the use of the opening, 'Chair'. That is present day left-wing Labourspeak, with no doubts intended. 'Mr Chairman' is equally, and unmistakably, to the right, but it may be excused in someone who is old and infirm. It is also tolerated from those increasingly few members of the party who have held high office. It is not welcome, but it is suffered. I did not at the time report the way in which Mr Smith began his speech to the rally, but I shall now. What he said was, 'Mr Chairman, comrades, and friends.' He had been Secretary of State in the Callaghan government, so the first mode of address was no more than could be expected, and was rendered more acceptable when modified by the two ambiguities which followed it.

Anyway, the man who began by saying simply, 'Friends,' was Mr Bill Jordan, President of the Amalgamated Union of Engineering Workers, who happens, on unilateralism for instance, to be on the far right, but who on the matter of the motor industry is in the Midland mainstream of the party. Birmingham, he said, had once been the engineering capital of the world, but now there were a third of a million unemployed in the west Midlands. Then it was he who went on to say: 'I grew up in it and saw its power. Some malice that we can't understand pulled it down.' And then he expressed a hatred of imports that was astonishing to hear. It amounted to xenophobia. He said the only boom was in the imports that filled the mushrooming supermarkets. And then to cars. 'We now have to move out of the way of these upmarket Japs and Germans . . . and our motor cars have been forced off the road by the four-wheeled paratroopers from Japan.'

The logical result of what Mr Jordan sincerely wants would be a kind of Yugoslavia where nothing that had been imported would be in the supermarkets, which would no longer mushroom, and indeed would often have very little in them at all.

The two MPs for West Bromwich, East and West, then spoke – Mr Peter Snape, who started as a railway clerk and later became a whip in the Callaghan administration, and Miss Betty Boothroyd, who was a member of the Tiller Girl dancing troupe in the 1940s before she went into politics. Miss Boothroyd said, 'We once had the highest income in England outside the south-east. Now it's plummeted.' Mr Snape said, 'This was once the heartland of Britain.' It was the same lament. But it was Mr Snape who returned to the poll at which Mr Smith had earlier hinted. He said there was a poll which showed the Tories with a lead reduced to two per cent. [Great excitement.]

'If we'd said a month ago that we'd be within an ace of

electing a Labour government, they'd have said it was a fantasy.'

Just so. Now that there was some hope, he could admit publicly what so many Labour politicians had thought privately until right up to the election – that there was no hope. But, more important, if that poll was right, then Labour was in with a chance. The rally ended on a high old note.

★   ★   ★

The Midland Hotel used to be the grand hotel of Birmingham. It was built next to the principal railway station, New Street. It used to have a solid grandeur: it now has four stars. To reach it, in the maze that is now the centre of Birmingham, you come out of the station, find your way into a vast shopping centre, cross that, go up an escalator, then descend precipitous steps, and you are at the back entrance. I was shown a room which the porter carrying my bag took one look at and himself described as a broom cupboard. I refused it, but accepted a second which would barely do. As you could tell from the irregular shape, it had probably been carved out of what was once a landing or corridor. Pigeon droppings had not been cleaned from the outside window sills. The hotel had a restaurant where the lamb was served overdone and where cheese turned up on your computerized bill as 'fromages'. I have known the Midland for many years. It has lost all tone, but then so has Birmingham. This is the city of Joseph Priestley, the cleric and chemist, the man who discovered, or at least first isolated, oxygen; of Matthew Boulton and James Watt, who made steam engines at the Soho foundry; of John Baskerville, the typefounder and printer; of John Bright the free-trader; and of Joseph Chamberlain, manufacturer of screws, a member of Gladstone's cabinet and later of Salisbury's, and a man who, as mayor of Birmingham, promised that in twelve months, with God's help, the town should not know itself, and thereupon rebuilt its centre on the grand scale. It is a city where almost all the good buildings are nineteenth century. Perhaps the finest is the town hall, which resembles a Greek temple: it was there that Mendelssohn conducted the first performance of 'Elijah' in 1847.

Alas, there came another time, from 1957 on, when the town once again learned not to know itself. The centre was torn apart and then reassembled as a pattern of concrete ramps and flyovers. All this is now heartily detested, but it is worth saying that, in the early 1960s, so sensitive and acute an observer and writer as Mr Geoffrey Moorhouse, seeing it all happening, and the bulldozers still present, liked what he saw. He then wrote, in his book *The Other England*, that nowhere in England was there more excitement in the air; there, possibly, was the most extensive redevelopment plan of any European city. I too was there at the time, working briefly on the *Birmingham Post*, which was then a newspaper with much the style and substance of the *Daily Telegraph*. Now it has been modernized into a tabloid.

Late that night, after the rally and after the Midland's dinner, I went for a walk in the city centre. It was a Friday night. Young people were out on the town. Not in the new town, though, whose concrete wastes were deserted. But in New Street there were crowds wandering about, window shopping, coming out of restaurants singing, coming out of pubs and being sick, and strolling up to the cathedral and Colmore Row, which is the handsome, Victorian part of town where the roads are wide, where the substantial buildings are now mostly banks, and where the night buses go from. That is why so many people were going that way. It is not quite what it was. Twenty years ago, even ten, the night buses, which left on the hour, were full at midnight, at one, and even at two in the morning. The bit of green round the cathedral used to be full of young men and girls chatting each other up in the light, or kissing in the dark. Then the buses would pull in. They seemed to have left the garage together, and to arrive at the bus station together. They would line up, about seven of them, one behind the other. Couples would scramble to get on, jumping over the low wall that separated the cathedral green from the pavement. Then, on the hour, there was a ritual race. At the first stroke, the drivers started up, the conductors rang bells, and off they went down a straight, wide, one-way street. All the buses were the same, so who led on this first stretch depended on the skill or recklessness of the driver. They took the first stretch fast because it was, I suppose, their only chance. After a quarter of a mile they separated, and then each dawdled off on its own route.

The buses are no longer run by Birmingham City Transport but by Midlands Travel. And there are fewer night buses now, on fewer routes. More young people have cars, even if they are made in Japan. But at midnight there were still hundreds of people standing or roaming around. The *Birmingham Evening Mail*, with twenty-six pages of job advertisements, was still on sale at one newsstand, which is a sign of life. In a concrete underpass under Corporation Street, a kiosk was scrawled all over with mysterious graffiti, like FRESH FORCE, and VICIOUS LGV + BONNIE TLE. A lone poster from the *Socialist Worker* gave this advice: 'Vote Labour but build a fighting socialist alternative.' That was exactly the support the Labour Party did not want at any price. Outside the Midland Hotel a policeman took no notice of a man standing crying against a wall, holding his hands up to his bloodied face.

Next morning, after a four-star breakfast of congealed fried eggs and cold toast, I negotiated the obstacle course back to New Street station and caught the London train. There was no mention in any of the half dozen newspapers I read of any poll showing that the Conservative lead had narrowed to two per cent, nor did I ever hear again of such a poll or such a result. But it had raised the spirits of Brierley Hill the night before.

ELEVEN

Our Lady of Finchley

By the last Saturday of the campaign the Conservatives had restored introductory music to their morning press conference in Smith Square, and very martial music it was. 'How I love the smell of napalm this early in the morning,' said an American reporter.

What that morning's press conference did not have was Mrs Thatcher. She was keeping herself in reserve for the rest of the day's electioneering, leaving Mr Tebbit in charge as Chairman and Mr Lawson, as Chancellor of the Exchequer, to provide the meat. Mr John Major, a junior minister from Social Security, was also, and surprisingly, present. They all sat under a slogan saying 'Down with Income Tax.' They were there to devote their energies to the taking apart of Labour's tax plans, insofar as these had ever been explained.

Mr Lawson started by saying that Labour's assertion that what you would get was what you saw in the manifesto just wasn't true. Nobody was surprised he should say this about Labour's manifesto, and everyone waited for more.

Mr Lawson: 'It's difficult to imagine anything more . . .'

Mr Tebbit: 'Deceitful?'

Mr Lawson: 'Yes, deceitful. I'm trying to moderate my language.'

Mr John Major, of whom few people had heard much, then mentioned a few figures of which nobody took much notice, and Mr Tebbit said he hoped that on Monday Mr

Hattersley would be able to produce a table to show who except the Duke of Westminster would have to pay Labour's higher taxes.

Another hiatus ensued. Mr Tebbit earlier mentioned that this was the last weekend conference of the campaign, for which we would all be grateful, and he was being proved right. He was being received with grateful silence. So he said that something was a smear from end to end, which raised a small laugh, and the whole thing pretty well fizzled out. Both Mr Tebbit and Mr Lawson were grateful for the questions of Miss Elinor Goodman of ITN's 'Channel 4 News', who that morning was the only reporter with much spirit left. Without Miss Goodman, the press conference would not have lasted the distance. And without Mrs Thatcher, the impetus was gone. The only reason some of the Press were there that morning was that they were due to travel round with the Prime Minister that day, and their bus would be leaving from Smith Square just after the conference.

It was a mystery tour. Throughout the campaign her people would not say until the last moment where she was going and when. With the IRA still out there, this was only sense. But you could get hints. It was known that this would be somewhere-in-north-London day, and, knowing that, you did not need to be a genius to guess that she would go to her own constituency at Finchley. And so it turned out. But first, the minders told us, we were going up to South Mimms on the M25. When we left Mr Lawson and Mr Tebbit and went out into the square, Mrs Thatcher's bus was waiting there with South Mimms written boldly on the side, and I wondered, not for the first time, how real all this security was. Anyone could have seen that bus standing there, read the sign, and had an hour's notice of the Prime Minister's destination.

The M25 is a fixation of Mrs Thatcher's. She had opened it herself the previous October. In her opening speech she had a hack at those who, she said, carped when they ought to be congratulating Britain and beating drums for Britain the world over. I will beat whatever drums I can for Britain. But with respect to the Prime Minister, the M25 was no matter for the beating of drums. It was a matter for asking what possible excuse there could be for a single tat-tat-tat for the timidity of the politicians and engineers who brought about such a work. There were 120 miles of it and it had taken fourteen years to build. Now how could a common or garden motorway, of that short distance, take so long? And why was it so absurdly far out from the centre of London – nearly twenty miles in places – something which must have been obvious even to those bicycling protectors of disused allotments who ensured that it should not be closer in? And what of the engineering? Some of the new bridges over the motorway are elegant, but most are not, and easily the most striking work on its whole length is a brick-built, nineteenth-century railway viaduct which crosses it south-east of Rickmansworth. And the journey from the ring road itself into London remains difficult and sordid. London still has the worst approach roads of any big city in the western world.

And all this was the sadder because it was England in the nineteenth century that was the home of audacious engineering. The English (and the Scots) built the railways of England, and of half the world besides, on a scale that would now amaze us. The London to Birmingham railway, which opened in 1838, was built in four years and is full of mighty works – bridges, viaducts, cuttings and tunnels – which are not demanded of a motorway engineer today. Cars can easily climb hills and take curves. An early locomotive could do neither, so the railway had to be built flat and straight. The line from London to Bristol was known as Brunel's billiard table because it had a mean gradient of one in 1,380.

The M25 was not a patch on the railways we had built 140 years before, and not a patch on roads the Americans were building around any of their big cities forty years before, and not a patch on the Paris périphérique. We had built a motorway round London, of only three lanes, and miles from where it was needed – and what was principally astonishing about that was the mangy poverty of our present expectations.

Now, since no one could characterize Mrs Thatcher's expectations as mangily poor, the only conclusion left was that she had rarely been driven on the road without its being cleared for her, and had certainly never driven on it herself, and could never have looked with any attention at a decent modern road either in Europe or north America. Even if all that was true, it remained a matter of amazement that she could still be lavishing praise on a road which so many people knew from their own experience to be second rate. But there she was that morning out at South Mimms, due to open the first service station and café on a road that had, again astonishingly, been built originally with no services on it at all.

'Look,' said the Central Office minder on the bus on the way out, 'we'll probably have her filling up our back-up Range Rover. You'll have to keep back fifteen paces. If Denis is with her you won't be able to separate them. We'll actually sus it out when we get there, OK? There's no end to the fun we bring you boys.'

The photographers on the bus were blasé. They'd seen it all before. Besides, they were more interested in swopping yarns about the forthcoming cost of their one-day swan to Venice to snap Mrs Thatcher in gondolas at the summit. Hotels had been demanding and getting £250 a night, and bowls of Venetian soup were estimated to cost £9 each.

When we got to South Mimms, the petrol filling opportunity was off. Security hadn't liked it. At his new caff, Lord Forte himself padded around talking anxiously to a man in a red coat who was to be the master of ceremonies. Flowers were piled up on a dais in front of the babies' changing room. After persistent enquiry these were identified for the press as Michaelmas daisies and lupins. Mr Cecil Parkinson and his wife entered, amid a buzz buzz of speculation. Was all forgiven? Would he be in again? Surely all was forgiven now?

Minder: 'She'll be going into the shop when she arrives.'

What shop?

'It's just called The Shop.'

And so it was, with a kids' corner, and a section for cash and wrap.

Then, at 11.20, ''Ere we go,' said the BBC1 cameraman. 'Here comes the old bitch,' said his colleague with the BBC2 team.

And Mrs Thatcher walked from her armour-plated bus into the caff, with a hand to her head to protect her hairdo against the strong wind. Lord Forte, much shorter than her, guided her in with his hand on her back.

'Pray silence,' said the man in the red coat.

Lord Forte, Charles Forte that was, began, 'Prime Minister, Your Excellency, Mr Parkinson, Mr Mayor – I think I shoud have started with that . . .?', and then, constantly wringing his hands, gratuitously confessed that it was twenty-five years since he opened his first caff on the M1, and asked God to bless Mrs Thatcher.

Nobody took much notice of him, and at about this time the reporters, who mostly had no idea where the place was on the map, suddenly twigged that South Mimms was in Mr Parkinson's own constituency, and that therefore his presence was routine and of no particular significance. This was a disappointment.

Then Mrs Thatcher, in a very good suit with the widest and most fashionable of shoulder pads, replied to Lord Forte, saying that the M25 was excellent, which was tosh, and that the caff around her couldn't have been built without the talents of Lord Forte. Might she say how much she loved his talent and ability? He had started with nothing. He could not have succeeded as he had unless he pleased the people he served, by giving good value and by producing what the people wanted. Governments could not create this sort of business: Lord Forte could. Everywhere she went round the world she found Trust House Forte hotels flying the flag. She was glad to open this great service area to add to all the good things on the M25.

She unveiled a plaque. Then she went into Julie's Pantry,

where a man made a bow so obsequious that it collapsed into a curtsey. The man in the red coat respectfully asked the Press to keep back, and they trampled over him. A salt-of-the earth lady from Central Office was much firmer and more successful with a French TV crew, driving them back before her. The French reporter, in a futile gesture of defiance, made as if to unzip the flies of his jeans, and she withered him with a look.

In a cafeteria called The Granary, Mrs Thatcher manifested intense interest in peanuts and smoked peppered mackerel, and a girl showed her how to fill a teapot with hot water. Thus instructed, Mrs Thatcher did it herself. 'What do you want?' she asked the assembled onlookers. 'Tea or coffee?' It was a teapot. 'That's lovely,' she said. A crash of crockery was heard as a TV crew climbed onto one of Lord Forte's stainless-steel work tops. Mrs Thatcher chatted with a check-out girl called Angela and then turned her attention to the pattern on Lord Forte's formica table tops.

'Look,' she said, 'there and on the carpet. It's the same pattern.'

Lord Forte expressed ready agreement.

'I'm sorry,' she said, 'I've learned to look at detail.'

Anna, a caff girl in uniform, was ushered forward to demonstrate the use of a plastic dustpan or suchlike.

'Absolutely vital,' said the Prime Minister, 'because I loathe going into a place where the tables aren't pristine. So you'll keep it clean to show all foreign travellers who come here how clean we are?'

The Press, having long before broken out of their red-roped pen, stampeded among the two palm trees and twelve kitschy lamp standards in the forecourt, and Mrs Thatcher departed for lunch where they couldn't get at her. Then Martin, a waiter or manager or something, assuaging the Press with champagne, let it drop that the supercaff had already been open for three weeks anyway.

We left, drove for a few mile back into suburban north London, past McDonald's, past Oddbins, and stopped for a pub lunch that in its squalor outcaffed the worst motorway caff you ever saw, (which would of course not be Lord Forte's,) where one woman served sandwiches and gave dirty change with the same hands. I asked a man with a pint if this wasn't Mrs Thatcher's own constituency. He said it was. We were in Finchley. He said he would vote for Maggie. I asked what he disliked about Labour: its defence policy, its solemnly promised tax increases, or what? He thought, and said, 'It's their attitude, isn't it?'

There was only one more engagement that day, Mrs Thatcher was giving herself a very easy time of it. Any incumbent Prime Minister can do that. She did not have to do as Kinnock, Owen and Steel were doing – slave round the country from six in the morning till midnight, exhausting themselves, their staff, and the Press. She was followed everywhere by twice the number of television crews that her opponents could command, and whatever she did was gratefully reported. Overheard scraps of her conversation were pounced upon – as I have pounced on the bits I heard – and cherished like relics. It is the iron rule of the market, that what is scarce is the more eagerly sought.

We went on to Avenue House, a Victorian mansion in baronial style erected by Henry Stephens (1841-1918), the man who made his fortune from Stephens' Ink. There, waiting in a large room with painted wooden beams and a stone fireplace, entertained by the strains of Mr Andrew Lloyd Webber's Tory theme tune that sounded like 'The Big Country', sat one hundred and fifty selected constituency loyalists. A man called Ron appeared, a local chairman, who told us the candidate had a hell of a schedule (which she hadn't). He then introduced the candidate, calling her, 'The Lady. Our Lady. Our Margaret', and asked for a big hand for our Denis too.

Our Lady of Finchley. Mrs Thatcher's minders kept their faces impassive, but if protocol allowed Central Office minders to speak, they would have put Ron down like a dog for providing headline fodder like that.

Then Mrs Thatcher made a short speech. Now she had nothing to gain from these people. They were all her supporters anyway, for whom her presence was meant as a reward. There were no television cameras because this was her own constituency and no channel could touch her there without giving equal time to her opponents in the Finchley election. There were not even any still photographers there. So there was no need for artifice.

What she gave in that room was a small demonstration of what she is and why she is leader of her party. I shall have to justify those words. No one of ordinary judgment can ever doubt that she means what she says, but it can sound awfully strident. This is almost always so in public, whether in Downing Street exhorting people to rejoice after the recapture of South Georgia, or at the Perth rally that began this campaign, or even at South Mimms telling Anna to keep the caff pristine. It is not in her to understate. Subtlety is not her strength. The glancing allusion is not for her. Nor do I want to suggest that she just chatted, even to her own people. She was still high-flown, and at the beginning a bit corny, saying it was good to come home after travelling all round the country. She was soon going to Venice. You needed to come home to gather strength. Yes, but Finchley wasn't home, just her constituency. She lived in Downing Street, and had lived before that in Chelsea.

But she spoke without a text, without notes, and she allowed herself gestures. She has good, actressly hands. When she makes a formal speech she always keeps them down. She was probably advised long ago to do that, because it looks neater that way on television. But that afternoon she was not on television, and she used her hands. She didn't shout. She said she was passionate about the election. In eight years Britain had turned round. Britain was trusted overseas. The country was strong and confident. The prospect of that being thrown away was appalling to her.

She talked about defence. If we had believed in peace at any price, Britain would have been defeated by tyrants long ago. There was something in this country which said, 'Stand up and fight.' Here she quoted Gaitskell, of all people, as saying he would fight and fight and fight again to save the party he loved from the unilateralists. And now, she said, the kind of people he had fought were leading the Labour Party. She said that Winston (I don't know how well she can have known Churchill, but she called him Winston) had said, 'Don't ever abandon that weapon.' She said that if Britain did, it wouldn't just be one more country giving up. 'It would be as if the cornerstone of European freedom cracked and collapsed.' She then went on about the winter of 1978-79, and the fraud of inflation which had eventually obliged us to go to the IMF like a Third World country. She said she felt this intensely strongly.

If that speech had been written for her, it would have pulled in a few tricks, but it would not have been so good. She didn't notice it, but on the wall hung a framed flag of the Middlesex Regiment, with its battle honours of Mysore, Albuera, Mons, and Inkerman. She was making a patriotic speech but did not mention, or I think remember, that it was the anniversary of D-Day. She would, perhaps, have been better if, instead of telling us she felt intensely, she had let her intensity speak for itself, but, as I have said, she hasn't much art as a speaker. But what she did have, and abundantly demonstrated as she spoke, was complete conviction. I never heard her speak better. I had no shadow of doubt that she meant it all. It was not possible to doubt her intention to preserve what she believed herself to have achieved. That is all: but these are great things.

There you are. She went off in her Daimler escorted by three Special Branch cars. One of her bodyguards that day was a woman who looked like a character on the wrong side in a James Bond film. The Press bus then got stuck in the drive, and in getting itself unstuck knocked down a one-way sign and destroyed ten feet of rose bushes. The Prime Minister had finished her day's electioneering at a quarter to three in the afternoon.

★　★　★

The next day, the last Sunday of the campaign, came the rally at Wembley conference centre, with laser beams, loads of dry ice, balloons, cacophony, and, in order of appearance, Bob Monkhouse, Schnorbitz the St Bernard dog, a cast of thousands, and, as the climax to the show, Margaret Thatcher. The 2,600 or so people in the audience had been carefully chosen. All had impeccable connections. I asked a few people at random why they were there. Two had tickets given to them by their constituency agent. One woman, who had also brought her two sons, had got tickets from her husband who worked at Central Office.

In 1983 it had been called a youth rally, and there were merry jokes about kicking Mr Foot's crutch away. In 1987 it was called a family rally, which meant smutty. Mr Bob Monkhouse told a joke. Glenys had known on her honeymoon that Neil would become Leader of the Labour Party because all he did was sit on the side of the bed and talk about how good things were going to be. Now it was fair enough for him to go on and say that Mrs Thatcher called Mr Kinnock Flash, because she liked to wipe the floor with him occasionally, but Kinnock is a word that lends itself to end-of-pier innuendo, and this was well exploited.

Mr Bernie Winters appeared with the dog Schnorbitz, and led the singing, with words projected on to a screen behind him, of 'Who do you think you are kidding, Mr Kinnock?' to the tune of 'Who do you think you are kidding, Mr Hitler?', that hit of the music hall season of 1939.

Then the celebrities were introduced one at a time – Mr Ronnie Corbett, Mr Adam Faith, Mr Clive Lloyd the great West Indian batsman, Ms Zandra Rhodes who designs dresses, England's number two badminton player, an ex-boxer, an all-in wrestler, and Ms Judith Chalmers, described on the handout as well-known. When a celebrity has to be described as well-known that is the kiss of death. I counted forty-one celebrities in all. I had never heard of twenty of them. Miss Shirley Bassey sent her apologies.

The massed Conservative families then sang along with Mr Errol Brown of the group Hot Chocolate as he led them in John Lennon's old song, 'Imagine'. '*Imagine no possessions*', sang these members of the property-owning democracy. '*I wonder if you can.*' I wondered if they knew what they were singing. Mr Stan Boardman, a Scouse comedian, had a go at both the Russians and the Irish. 'Gorbachev doesn't want to take over the world? Of course he bloody does. He's got a map of it tattooed on his head.' And then: 'The Irish invented the lavatory seat but the British took over and improved it by putting a hole in it.'

This pattern repeated itself. I cannot remember which comic cracked the same joke about Gorbachev's map of the world, nor who it was that said his dad was Irish and had got a good job as rear gunner on a milk float. Then Jan Leeming, the former newsreader, described in the handout as definitely *not* retired, was received with ecstasy and recited with deep bathos the statement, in itself dignified, in which Sir Yehudi Menuhin had a few days before condemned the Labour Party.

It is difficult to explain how dreadful all this was. It was all so wrong in tone, so bad of its kind, so naff.

Then came the laser show, played to the deafeningly jazzed up chords of 'Jerusalem' reproduced by some organ or synthesizer. Then Mr Tebbit wheeled his wife on to the stage, and then Mrs Thatcher appeared.

'Denis tells me', she said, 'that the music for that song you just sang was the signature tune for 'Dad's Army'. Well, I don't know about 'Dad's Army'. But I'm a *Mum* and I like to think that those who believe in keeping Britain strong, free and properly defended belong in *Mum's* Army.' Then more of the same. 'The Leader of the Labour Party even talks about occupation. Occupation? Occupation of Britain? After winning two world wars without a single enemy soldier on British soil?' [Cheers.]

Defence was the single strongest point of her entire campaign, and had been throughout, and she threw it away in a rant. The great rally had been two hours of smutty jokes, baying, braying, and then a fair old rant. Nothing I had ever seen in the grubbiest of American elections touched its depths.

So what was to be made of it? There on Saturday was Mrs Thatcher in her own constituency speaking with conviction and carrying conviction. The next day, there she was taking part in a degraded circus. 'It lifts the heart', she said, 'to hear the Wembley roar.'

But it does not. She arrived only at the end of the rally. It may have been that she did not hear the awfulness that went on before. But, as she herself said, this was the third rally she had held at Wembley on the Sunday before an election.

What *was* to be made of it all? There, I suggest, were the two aspects – the one on show on Saturday, the other on Sunday – of Our Lady of Finchley. You buy one, you buy the other.

TWELVE

Pharaoh's Ants and Vows of Silence

After the rally, Mrs Thatcher had finished with the demotic for a while, and went off to Venice to be photographed in gondolas. Meanwhile, the Conservative headquarters in Hackney North had been burned out. Petrol was splashed on the stairs. Police said it was arson. The Tories lost thousands of leaflets and the registers of their supporters. The fire was set at night, and was first seen at three o'clock in the morning. No one was hurt, though the occupants of the house next door had to be moved.

It was a dismal sight next morning, in a dismal part of London. The headquarters was in a decrepit eighteenth-century house opposite a row of seedy shops. 'Smart Wear' sold second-hand clothes. 'Movies Center' hired out videos, but was closed down, with grilles over all the windows. Mr Tebbit came to see the damage at lunchtime, and was told it was arson. 'Well,' he said, 'if that's what the evidence points to it's a very sad moment, to find that politics has got down to arson.'

Did he think it was the work of his political opponents? 'I don't think it's the work of my political friends. One can only assume that if it is arson it was an outrage perpetrated by the extreme Left. I don't know whether by members of the Labour Party, or the SWP (Socialist Workers' Party), or anything else. But what I do know is that all of us in democratic parties would deplore this sort of thing. I'm sure

Mr Kinnock would deplore this extremely vigorously. I
recollect his vigorous denunciation of the violence during
the coal strike.' It was a fair crack.

It also made good television. Police and firemen were still
sifting around in the sodden wreckage. On the ground were
scattered the cards of a salvage service: 'DISASTER CALL: Fire,
Flood, Crime. Any other Disasters. 24 Hours a Day. Back
in Business in Hours.' And there was Mr Tebbit's gaunt
face with a ruined building in the background. You did not
need a long political memory to remember him being dug
out of the ruins of the bombed Metropole in Brighton, also
on television.

There was no real evidence who did it. But just down the
road, Anarchist posters were pasted on walls. One said
'Never trust a politician. They always lie.' Another, which
showed a Rolls Royce being bashed in, said, 'Let's kick out
the Tories, Let's kick them in.' And before Mr Tebbit had
arrived, the Conservative candidate, inspecting the ruins,
had said he didn't think the fire was the work of any of the
main political parties. There were, he said, a lot of lunatics
in Hackney, the fringe of a fringe.

The electoral contest continued. Three bricks were hurled
at the window of the Labour offices. The Conservatives
took refuge in an anonymous and unmarked house whose
address was not published, but whose telephone number
was available on request.

Wanting to see more of the constituency, I asked Conservative Central Office for that number. 'Let me see,' said
the voice at the other end of the line. 'Hackney. That'll be
north London?'

I then asked both the Conservative and Labour agents if
I could go canvassing with their candidates, to see what they
and their electors were like. They were unusual candidates.
Mr Oliver Letwin, the Tory, was thirty-one, a Fellow of
Darwin College, Cambridge, and a member of the Prime
Minister's policy unit. Those of his election leaflets which
had survived the fire stated that he was descended from
refugees who fled from communism during the Russian

revolution. They did not state that he was a merchant banker or that he had been to school at Eton. He was a very good candidate, who would go places, but not that time. He was fighting his first campaign in the traditional impossible seat. The Labour candidate was Miss Diane Abbott, aged thirty-three, of Newnham College, Cambridge, and formerly of the Home Office, Thames Television, TV-am and the GLC. If she was elected, she would become the first black woman MP.

Mr Tebbit had already brought Miss Abbott's political views to the notice of the House of Commons two years before, when he quoted from a 'policy document' of which she was one of the signatories. The text read: 'We are not interested in reforming the prevailing institutions – the police, armed forces, judiciary, and monarchy – through which the ruling classes keep us in "our place". We are about dismantling them and replacing them with our own machinery of class rule.' Miss Abbott had also been indiscreet enough to tell a woman's magazine that her favourite moment had been making love to a naked man in a Cotswold hayfield – but that was only human, and probably redounded to her credit. In his two election pamphlets Mr Letwin went for her hard. In one he asked directly: 'Do you really want Diane Abbott as your MP?' In another, he reproduced facsimilies of newspaper reports quoting her as saying all white people were racist, and that Militant was right-wing. Opposite these quotations there was a drawing of Labour's red rose, from the stalk of which flew a hammer and sickle flag, with the caption, 'Many people have forgotten that the hand that clutches a red rose also brandishes a red flag.' And, underneath, 'Don't let the red flag fly over your local police station.' In return, Miss Abbott's office put out a notice that she had 'instructed her solicitors to take action over libel statements'. Mr Letwin took legal advice of his own and continued to distribute the pamphlets. He never received a writ, and after the first solicitor's letter heard nothing more.

I took a taxi to meet Mr Letwin. As we entered the London borough of Hackney, which announced on signposts that it had declared itself a nuclear-free zone, the driver of taxi 5787 had a variation on the party political statements of his colleagues. He said that in many parts of London the public lavatories were disappearing. It was the fault of the councils. But, he said, there was an ancient law, dating from horse-cab days and as yet unrepealed, which allowed drivers to urinate against the back wheel. If a policeman was there he was supposed to hold his cape so as to shield you from public view.

Hackney has come down in the world. It used to be in the country. Samuel Pepys went there to take the air and to shoot with bow and arrows. Daniel Defoe called it a remarkable retreat for wealthy citizens. There is still a Defoe Road, and a plaque to Defoe, but just round the corner from that stands a shop with second-hand gas cookers displayed for sale on the pavement outside.

Mr Letwin was being helped in his campaign by his academic colleagues. On a sofa in his new headquarters lay an essay on Henryson and the other Scottish followers of Chaucer. His own election pamphlet described him as having been a university lecturer. I asked in what. He said philosophy. He had written a book called *Ethics, Emotion, and the Unity of the Self*, which was soon to be published.

We went out canvassing. He attached a loudspeaker to the roof of his Saab 900, we set off, and he started broadcasting. 'The last four days of Labour rule in Hackney,' he said over and over again through his loudspeaker as we went along. Thirty per cent of the voters in his constituency are black or Asian. A few young blacks gave him dismissive waves, but that was all. Hackney also has one of the largest populations of Hassidic Jews outside New York or Jerusalem. There are believed to be 12,000 in the borough, and about 6,000 in Hackney North. We first went canvassing in a Jewish area, where the people were Conservative to a man and a woman. They are travel agents, accountants, and property men, not all rich but few of them poor. Mr Letwin said he had trouble remembering that it wasn't done to offer to shake hands with an Orthodox Jewish woman. This was awkward, since it is a gesture that comes instinctively to a canvassing candidate. He said the Hassidic Jews used not to be so politically solid, or politically active at all. Many emigrated from Germany and eastern Europe in the 1930s, and were for many years afterwards afraid to take any part in politics. In election after election they did not vote at all. They do now.

I asked what had happened to the intellectual Jewish vote of the sixties, which was for Labour. He said it had crumbled. In half an hour only one man failed to promise his support. 'Scum,' he said. 'You're for the rich, not the poor.' But otherwise the support was universal. I asked if we could find something else.

'There's a nasty down there,' said Mr Letwin, and we set course for a small tower block of council flats. The one lift did not work and had not worked for weeks. On the landings, smashed windows had been left unrepaired for months. It should have been solid Labour territory, but it was not. Mr Letwin knocked on dark doors which opened off obscure balconies. Occasionally there was some movement inside but the door remained closed. One door had a notice saying, 'Calls only by arrangement or appointment.' People were afraid of being mugged.

But when the doors were opened, three people in a row said they had voted Labour before, but would vote for Letwin this time. Now some people will tell a candidate anything to get rid of him, but this is usually done shiftily, seldom with conviction, and never in my experience by people who give reasons. These people gave reasons.

'They're not really Labour,' said one woman. 'It's a different kind.'

'Let me have a look at you,' said one man on a murky balcony. 'All right. I'll be there on Thursday.'

'You see the colour of my face?' said one elderly white man. 'That's where I'll be voting.'

Mr Letwin protested, 'Not for that reason.' But it was a vote he had, like it or not.

The woman next door gave him another reason. Would she vote for him? 'Wouldn't be at all surprised. Get rid of the Queen! I always voted Labour before.' Miss Abbott's reputation had preceded her, though a bit garbled.

In the streets a few people yelled at Mr Letwin to fuck off, but probably the most frequent response he got when he knocked on doors was that people did not know, or care. Several stated definitely that they were not going to vote at all. But again, people in pitiful high-rise blocks wished him luck. 'And this', he said, 'is a safe Labour seat?'

Had anyone ever told him they were going to vote Alliance? 'They haven't heard of it,' he said. 'The likes of you and me vote Alliance.'

Then we arrived at a grubby block of council flats called the Northwold estate. Parked in the courtyard were an L-registered Mercedes, an R-registered Rover, and two newer Golfs. Mr Letwin saw a young black man and pursued him to seek his vote.

The man looked at him: '*She* says on TV that she will spend her money as she wants, have what treatment she wants. All right, she can do it. But how many can?' He waited.

'But it doesn't hurt you if she does,' said the candidate, enquiring again after the man's vote.

'I'm heartbroken to take it from you,' said the man, with dignity. 'But no.'

He would be voting Labour, then?

The man thought: 'I shall not vote at all.'

Here was a man who was lucid, who gave a real reason for not voting Conservative, but who, after consideration, was not going to vote at all. The turnout in Hackney North had been traditionally low, but it looked as though it would be even lower this time.

I asked Mr Letwin what he really thought about his Labour opponent, and he did not know. 'Who is the real Diane Abbott?' he said. 'Far left? Or Kinnock-like? I don't know.'

It was impossible to tell from Miss Abbott's own election publications. Her formal pamphlet, expensively printed with three four-colour photographs, did not say a single word, one way or the other, about Militant, or the dismantling of the police, the judiciary, and the monarchy. The newsletter of her constituency party published recommendations for Miss Abbott from actresses in the TV soap 'EastEnders' and in the West End musical of *Edwin Drood*. The superintendent of the Methodist church at Stoke Newington was quoted as saying that Labour was the party of the poor, the 'marginated', the powerless, and the voiceless. There was even an appeal to vote Labour from a Hackney Liberal candidate in the 1979 general election.

On the telephone, the workers at her committee rooms had been unencouraging and evasive. So after I left Mr Letwin I just went along there and asked if I could go canvassing with her. This is an ordinary request. Her agent, Mr John Burnell, suggested that if I wanted to meet voters I should try the streets. I said what I wanted to see was Miss Abbott at work. Mr Burnell was put out that I should have come at all, and then explained, as he previously had on the telephone, that this would be considered an intrusion; that Miss Abbott's canvassing was one-on-one; that it was confidential between her and her constituents. All right, did he himself, as agent, think it true that more people simply weren't going to vote at all this time? Mr Burnell introduced a young black man to answer for him. He was a man of great persuasive charm. He said the particularity of this situation was that people were not afforded an opportunity to fulfil their roles. He spoke with fluency the language of the left-wing seminar. Yes, I said, but about the numbers who might not vote? He replied – I condense his reply – that the young were cynical and the older people disillusioned. Blacks, he said, were not a homogeneous class.

Then, Miss Abbott herself came in, and I asked her for a few words. She smiled, and immediately went into the back of the shop, and sat where we could see each other through a large window. I waited. The committee rooms were in a second-hand bookshop, whose profits, I was told, helped out the party funds. There were novels by Hugh Walpole, Ben Travers, and Clive Cussler round the walls. The agent pressed pamphlets on me, one saying that if the fire at the Conservative headquarters had been started deliberately, then Miss Abbott condemned it as a cowardly act, and that in a democracy politics were conducted through the ballot box.

Look, I said, her opponent had shown me his view of the constituency. Wouldn't she show me hers? If she wouldn't, would she at least tell me that herself? I caught Miss Abbott's eye through the window. She gave me a full, frank, and free smile, then waved, and then turned away. She had inherited a majority of 8,545. She was said to have ten cars to Mr Letwin's one to take her supporters to the poll. Miss Abbott – Newnham, The Home Office, and Thames TV – was the only parliamentary candidate I had met in twenty-four years who had taken a vow of silence.

The only one, that is, until the next day.

★ ★ ★

Between Hackney Marshes and the higher parts of Greenwich, across the Thames, there is nothing to stop the northerly wind on a cold day, and some of Greenwich's tower blocks had been architect-designed in innocence of this essential fact.

Within the boundaries of Greenwich lie the Naval College, the old royal observatory, the meridian line dividing the world into east and west, the Queen's House, the Cutty Sark, and then the working-class tower blocks and pre-war tenements of the unprosperous parts of the constituency. Greenwhich had been Labour since the end of the war. Until 1971 the member was Richard Marsh, who became chairman of British Rail. His successor was Guy Barnett. As late as the time of Mr Barnett's death at the end of 1986, Greenwich looked a seat that Labour would have difficulty in losing. It was true that in 1982 Labour had lost Bermondsey to the

Alliance in a disastrous by-election, and that Bermondsey was only just along the river. In 1983 the SDP held Bermondsey in the general election. Guy Barnett's majority in Greenwich that time was not much over a thousand. The close runner-up was the Conservative. But still, only by really putting its mind to it could Labour lose Greenwich. Labour did put its mind to it. After bitter quarrels within the constituency and nationally, a Labour candidate was chosen who succeeded in losing Greenwich in the by-election of February 1987. Greenwich contains large parts of middle-class Blackheath. In Blackheath, if not in Hackney, they had heard of the SDP. The Laodicean professional men and women of Blackheath were confronted on the one hand by a Labour candidate of the far left, and on the other by what they saw as the excesses of Thatcherism. They thereupon elected to Parliament, by a majority of 6,611, the unknown and then famous Rosie Barnes of the SDP. When the general election came only four months later, the constituency Labour Party, showing less sense than loyalty to is disastrous by-election candidate, readopted that same candidate. Ms Deirdre Wood stood again.

I went to her committee rooms, and there, for the second time in two days, heard a familiar patter. Ms Wood's canvassing, said her agent, was one-on-one, and considered confidential, and therefore . . .

Now this is not only nonsense but instantly recognizable nonsense. Canvassing is not a confessional. Canvassing has to be quick: hullo, hand extended, vote for me, nice to meet you, goodbye, and then a fast exit remembering to close the garden gate. But on two consecutive days I was given the same non-reasons on behalf of two left-wing Labour candidates, and in almost the same words. But the new order had bitten less deeply in Greenwich. The agent might trot out the same words, but he was a less than wholehearted believer in the great Press Conspiracy theory, and though he would protect his candidate, as I guessed he had been told to, he also did what he had probably been doing for years and asked me upstairs for a cup of tea. Upstairs was the friendly confusion of an old-time Labour committee room – a few posters, piles of envelopes, people answering telephones and not caring if they were overheard. One call was about a family who had come down from the north and were living in a car: it was hoped that the council would find them a flat, even though they were what is known in local authority terms as intentionally homeless. The constituency workers talked about their late member, Guy Barnett. A man asked me if I had seen the Alliance poster showing the two Davids, with the caption, 'The Only Fresh Thing on the Menu'. I said I had. 'No meat and two veg,' he said. [Laughter.] Then the agent said that Mr Chris Fay, a Greenwich councillor and vice-chairman of the social services committee, would show me round the constituency if I liked.

We started out in Humber Road, which was still bedsit land. There had been 6,000 bedsits a few years before. Now there were only 2,000. Then Ulundi Road. The houses looked 1890s but were probably a bit earlier. Ulundi was a village in Natal where Lord Beresford defeated the Zulus in 1879 in one of those little wars that the British Empire was always winning or losing. In Ulundi Road there were a lot of 'miscellaneous acquired', which meant that houses had been bought by the council in the 1960s and divided into flats. Then we came to the Beaconsfield estate, where the name was no guide at all since the flats had been built in 1953, coronation year. A few years later and they would have been built of concrete and by now falling apart. As it was they were in the style of the 1930s, that is to say with metal windows and lots of glass, and with an underlying assumption on the part of the architect that England is a warm country. This makes them freezing cold to live in. The only heating is by gas fire, and, though the flats are not that high, the wind from Hackney Marshes gets them, and in winter the lace curtains freeze to the inside of those metal-framed windows. Still, they are your better class of council flat. Outside in the courtyard is a huge tree, called the King's Oak, believed to be eight hundred years old and to have stood there when the land was part of the King's park at Greenwich.

People had lived in these flats since they were opened, with optimism and altruism, in coronation year. One of the oldest residents was Mrs Doreen Williams. She was cheerful, though the flat had given her no end of trouble the previous winter. The tanks had frozen upstairs, then burst, and the water had come down, flooding everything, ruining her walls and her carpets. The ceilings had come down. Her oldest daughter, living in New Zealand, had an earthquake the same day as she had the flood.

How had she come to live in a council flat? She said she and her husband had always rented privately, until they were bombed out in the war, and then the council rehoused them.

Had she thought of voting SDP? She gave a comprehensive answer. 'I come from South Wales. I remember the 1930s. And my father always stuck up for Lloyd George.'

Mr Fay was looking around the redecorated flat with some pleasure. He said that on his council committee they usually saw the wallpaper only in samples. It was good to see it up, a whole room papered with it, so that you could really see what it was like.

Then we met Mr Fred Webb. 'The SDP? I hate David Owen. He's a renegade. He should have stayed and fought.' This was the authentic sound of the old Labour Party. There is no other party which so cherishes its traitors. Ramsay MacDonald, and now David Owen, are those they have in mind when they sing those two lines of 'The Red Flag':

> *Though cowards flinch and traitors sneer*
> *We'll keep the red flag flying here.*

Mr Webb had some scorn for Roy Jenkins too. 'Went off to the Common Market, that job. Didn't get offered a good enough job when he came back, so he and the other chap started their own business.'

As we left the Beaconsfield estate, Councillor Fay said people there reliably voted Labour. It was on the big estates like Ferrier where there was trouble in that way, and that was because those big estates were themselves trouble, some of them falling apart. He lived on the Ferrier estate himself, which was the biggest. It was named after Kathleen Ferrier, the great contralto. His own flat was on Telemann Square, which he said was named after the German composer. The parts of the estate were all named after musicians. He knew about the estate's 7,000 residents, its twelve tower blocks, its third-storey walkways which were a gift to muggers and other criminals, and its crumbling brown asbestos. He said that half the families on the estate had only one parent. Half? Yes, because the estate used to belong to the GLC, which had made it a policy to send women there who were unmarried or had been deserted, along with their children. The baby Kimberley, who had been beaten to death, had come from Ferrier. They'd had three such deaths in the last three years.

This vast and awful place – worse than the towers of Sheffield which are at least on hills – was built only in the early 1970s. In the last three years, seventeen million pounds had been spent trying to repair it. To put it really right was impossible, and anyway would cost more than to pull it down. It is a horrible place. It was obvious from everything that Mr Fay said that he minded about its awfulness, and about the people who had to live there. As a Labour supporter he also had quite a different trouble, which was that the residents had tended to vote against Labour in protest, because Greenwich was a Labour council. At the by-election which Rosie Barnes won, he reckoned that one in ten of the people from Ferrier voted SDP.

We went past the day nursery, which had wire mesh over the windows because they had been smashed so often, and then up to the New Horizons Centre. Mr Fay was proud of this. He told me that Deirdre Wood had opened it two years before, when she was with the GLC. Would I like to go inside and meet some people?

At the door we were repulsed. A woman in jeans saw us coming, opened the glass door slightly, and said, peremptorily, 'Woman's Day.' Mr Fay was clearly unhappy, but said nothing. I asked the woman – just making small talk in order to stay there for a moment and get a glimpse of what she was so intent on excluding us from – how often they held their women's days. She looked hard at me and said: 'I'm not prepared to comment. We have been told not to talk to reporters.' She closed the door. I looked at a poster on the door spelling out the word Welcome in many languages, remembering the last such poster I had seen, in Brent. Welcome and Beware. As I counted the number of languages – and this time there were twenty-four – the woman watched me implacably from behind her glazed door. Another vow of silence.

Watched all the way, Mr Fay and I walked away from the New Horizons Centre, past the Wat Tyler pub where there's a lot of broken glass on Friday and Saturday evenings, and then we caught sight of a poster propped up outside the rent office. It read:

WE'LL BUG YOU

UNTIL YOU

DE-BUG US

It was a sit-in. The rent office was occupied by about a dozen angry men and women, accompanied by children. Inside was a kiosk where rents were supposed to be paid, but this had been closed because the council feared for the safety of the clerk taking the rents. I can't think why. The sitters-in were angry, but they were going to harm nobody. They waved bottles of varying sizes at me, to demonstrate the contents. The largest bottle contained cockroaches, the middle-sized one carpet bugs, and the small one some other unidentified lice. One of the women had a reference book with pictures of insects, with which she supported her identification of the specimens. What they didn't have there to show me were the Pharoah's ants which were the greatest bane. These ants were small, red, and plentiful, but too agile to catch. They were said to invade the flats through the cracks in the walls. They would creep into a baby's nappy and chew at the child's bare flesh. They could even bite their way into tins of baked beans. I didn't believe this, but was assured it was so.

There was no vow of silence here. Names were pressed on me. Carol Monkhouse said her daughter was called fleabag at school because she was covered in bites, so she had refused to strip down to do gym. Sharon Ede said the Pharoah's ants could swarm into a woman's bed. Woman exhibited bitten and scratched limbs.

Then they complained about the rents they had to pay – £48 for a two-bedroom maisonette, £35 for a one-bedroom flat. I didn't say it seemed cheap, but I suppose my expression showed something of the sort because one man told me: 'This is a disaster area. No one wants to come and live here.' And it was true that I had seen that some of the flats were boarded up as I walked round the estate.

I asked them what they were going to do. The reply was unanimous and instant: 'We're withholding our votes.'

But who from? From which party?

'Who got in last time?' asked a man. 'Now you've got your answer.' I doubted if I had. Only half the estate had voted at the by-election anyway. That dreadful estate was the original work of the GLC. It was now being incompetently managed by a Labour-controlled Greenwich council, which claimed bitterly in its turn that a malicious Tory government was starving it of funds. But funds to do what? The estate was depressing, but not so depressing as those who lived there. They were, in sociologist's jargon, the marginated. Take all the helpless, the feckless, the worn-down-with-children, put them together in one ghetto, accustom them to rely on a council which no longer had the means or the will or the get-up-and-go to do much for them beyond providing that crumbling ghetto – and those were the men and women you would produce. In many cities all over the warm parts of the world, ants will swam over a grape which is left in the middle of a table. In New York or any other big American city, cockroaches infest kitchens in the summer. It is not beyond the wit of man to deter the ants and exterminate the cockroaches. You pour boiling water over the ants and poison the roaches. But these people at Ferrier were as hopeless, and for the most part as property-less, as refugees. They were people who all their lives had been taught that the State, or the council, owed them a living. It was hardly their fault that they continued in this debilitating belief.

The women who were withholding their votes held up a petition for me to see, signed with the childlike signatures of a thousand people. These were also the people who had been half-educated, if that, in schools which had fashionably demanded nothing of them. As I left they waved other bottles at me – bottles containing valium to sooth them by day and sleeping tablets for the nights.

Mr Fay continued the tour. We drove out of the estate into pleasant and gentrified Blackheath, where live the middle classes who are fortunate enough to be able to get themselves a decent living by their own wits. Their whole interest lay in voting Conservative, but something – perhaps, for the moment, merely another fashion – was inducing them to vote SDP. I reckoned that SDP posters in windows outnumbered Tory posters by eight to one. As Mr Fay said, that part of Blackheath was only a few minutes' drive from Ferrier, but it could have been a million miles. He said there had been a proposal, which failed, to build a brick wall to separate Ferrier from the road we had taken as we left. I would have called Mr Fay a Labour man of the old school, but he supported and liked Deirdre Wood, and resented outside attempts to dissuade the Greenwich Labour Party from choosing her. He said Rosie Barnes was by then treated with scepticism on the estates because she didn't know the Housing Acts, or the estates themselves for that matter.

Well, neither did I. In the 1970s I lived for a couple of years within half a mile of the Ferrier estate, and never knew it existed.

THIRTEEN

Last Trumpets from the Temperance Band

On the Tuesday before polling day the Alliance gave itself its last send-off, and put a brave face on it. The place chosen for this last rally was the Central Hall, Westminster, a great, domed place owned by the Methodists, just across the road from Westminster Abbey. At the beginning, it was a temperance band that played the Alliance signature tune, Purcell's trumpet tune No. 4. Mr Bamber Gascoigne, once more chairman or question master, said that time would add to that tune a golden tinge of nostalgia.

First there were the familiar trappings of the entrance of the two leaders. Television crews, for the last time, walked backwards before Dr Owen and Mr Steel as they processed the length of the aisle together, towards the platform. Then Mr Steel spoke first. Out electioneering that day he had as good as admitted that Mrs Thatcher would win an outright majority. That evening he said that Mr Kinnock could not win. By Friday morning, when they had counted the votes, Mr Kinnock with his red rose symbol would be remembering a line of William Blake's which went, 'O rose, thou art sick'. Then there would be an ever more divided nation. He spoke about the icy blast of disapproval from the Tory thought-police. It seemed that this blast would blow principally on the universities, civil servants, and the BBC. Nobody in the hall called out, 'And a good thing, too.' These Alliance rallies were open. Anyone could walk in, but those who did were almost always the faithful. Few infidels attended. Mr Steel said that then, when this icy blast blew, the chairman of the Conservative Party would never be off the broadcasters' backs: the Tory government hated the BBC. Then he had a crack at credit cards and increasing consumer debt, saying that if Mrs Thatcher had been captain of the *Titanic* she would have reassured passengers that the ship had only stopped to take on ice. [Laughter.]

Now this was all very well, but that joke went back at least to the October election of 1974 when Harold Wilson was making it known that if he was returned there wasn't going to be an economic crisis, or not a big one. Then it was the *Daily Telegraph* which said of him that if he had been captain of the *Titanic*, and so on. The *Titanic* is the most enduring modern image of disaster. When in 1973 President Nixon was drifting ever nearer to impeachment over Watergate, as far distant a newspaper as the *Honolulu Post* printed a cartoon showing Captain Nixon vainly throwing overboard from the foundering *Titanic* first of all his closest advisors (Haldeman and Ehrlichman), then the tapes of his White House conversations, and then the financial details which he had omitted from his tax returns. The very morning of the day that Mr Steel told his *Titanic* joke, the ever-moderate Mr Joe Haines, writing in the *Daily Mirror* under the headline 'Dirty Liars', said that the Tory campaign was sloshing its way through the sewers and that Lawson, Tebbit, Young, Hurd, and particularly Mrs Thatcher had fought the campaign 'like passengers fought for seats in the *Titanic*'s lifeboats'.

Leaving maritime disasters behind, Mr Steel then went on to say, 'We have sounded our trumpets at the walls of the two-party system, and they are crumbling before our eyes.' Even from his assembled supporters, there was only half-hearted applause for this. He went on unabashed to talk about the sweet smell of success, and to say that the time had come.

Messages of goodwill were then read out from the usual people concerned with entertainment: this time from

Richard Attenborough, Robert Powell, Denis Quilley, and
David Puttnam – *Chariots of Fire*, which he produced, thus
being seen to distribute its favours equally between the
Labour and Alliance Parties. He and Mr Hugh Hudson, the
director of that film, had both made their money in the big
bad market, for which neither of them at election time had
a good word to say.

It was then the turn of Dr Owen, who repeated, again
without a shred of evidence, that this was a thoughtful
election. He *shuddered* at the prospect of another four years
of Mrs Thatcher. But it was not inevitable that she would
win: even at that late hour people might change their minds.
People, he said, would vote for Mrs Thatcher more out of
fear than enthusiasm. He then said, twice, that we had
nothing to fear but fear itself; but he did so without attribu-
ting this remark to Roosevelt, as Mr Livingstone had done
at Brent earlier in the campaign. I shall return in the next
chapter to this idea of Fear.

Dr Owen then said there could be no 'deep democracy'
until there was proportional representation. There is no
subject in a British election more likely to lull an audience
to sleep, but it did rouse the only heckler of the evening to
shout out, 'What about the French?'

I have no reason to think this question was planted, but
nothing could have been more congenial to Dr Owen. This
is one of his favourite topics. Twenty years ago, he said,
twenty-five years ago if you liked, that would have been
fair enough. But now both France and Germany had a higher
standard of living than Britain. Last year, even Italy had
achieved a higher standard of living than us. This is a
comparison Dr Owen makes whenever he can. The British
decline riles him.

Anyway, he said, the virtue of PR was that it would force
parties to work together. Yes, the other parties said they
wouldn't talk to the Alliance, but they would talk. There
was still time, even under the present system, to make sure
of enough Alliance seats to force Mrs Thatcher to listen.

'Vote', he said, 'with the courage of your convictions,

with your head, and with your heart. In the remaining hours we must win the hearts of the people of this country. We can do it. Go to it.'

Even in those last hours Dr Owen could still command attention and applause, and he got both.

More messages were then read out from John Cleese, Ludovic Kennedy, Steve Race, and Julian Glover. It is a curious custom this, common to all parties. But who cares about the political opinions of these people? And if they wish the party so well, why aren't they there?

Then came the questions from the floor and we were into the distant yonder. Dr Owen was evidently willing to negotiate with anyone, and to compromise if necessary. Mr Steel, on the other hand, would not go in with anyone else's government unless it stuck to his principles. Then we entered fairyland itself. What if the Chiefs of Staff were to recommend unanimously that the order for Trident shoud be maintained? That was not, said Mr Steel, a matter he would even put to the Chiefs of Staff at all.

Well, no, he wasn't likely to.

Mr John Pardoe then made a speech. He is known as a fiery orator. Years before, he fought Mr Steel for the Liberal leadership, and lost. Then, in 1979, he lost his seat in Parliament. Now he said that without the Alliance there would be a choice only between two parties, and what a cabined, cribb'd, confined choice that would be – a choice between the Nanny State and a Governess in Westminster. The image of Mrs Thatcher as governess was a frequent one during the campaign. Mr Pardoe then said Mrs Thatcher claimed God was a Conservative. Mr Pardoe's manner suggested that he doubted if God was. Then he told an involved story that demonstrated that he (Pardoe) did not think Labour could rely on God's endorsement either. God would not, as it were, be sending messages to either of the two old parties, both of which were a bad lot. The gist of the story he told was this. I paraphrase and abbreviate it, but here it is. A young couple went to this left-wing castle where they were met by a suave butler. There was a play

here on the butler's name, whether it was Ghoul or Gould;
Bryan Gould, I suppose. The friendly host appeared, and
the young couple were offered sherry. But then, at full
moon, the coffin lids slid off and vampires came forth.
[Some applause.] Mr Pardoe then remarked that the curse
of a Labour government was that the leader had to spend so
much time protecting his back that he could not look the
nation in the face. He then said with bustling confidence
that a 'Newsnight' poll that very night would show that
David Owen was right, and that there would be a balanced
Parliament. I did not see that poll. Never once in the campaign did I hear a rumour about a poll which turned out
right.

To wind things up, Purcell's trumpet tune No. 4 was then
played again by the temperance band. The faithful left.
Upstairs, the Alliance stall was still trying to sell yellow
Proportional Representation ties, £4.50 each. Down the
marble stairs of the Central Hall, in the lobby, next to the
Coke machine, was this poster:

Election Day 1987

THE CHAPEL
WILL BE OPEN
ALL DAY
FOR PRAYER

Third Floor

FOURTEEN

The Taste of Fear and the Workers' Beer

I have never understood Mrs Thatcher, and do not remember anyone who was certain he did. But there is no getting away from the fact that she dominates political life. The constitutional convention is that a Prime Minister is merely *primus inter pares*. Things have, however, changed since Bagehot wrote his *English Constitution* in 1867. The reality is that a Prime Minister now has every opportunity to dominate. But no Prime Minister in recent history has dominated her colleagues, and the government of the country, as Mrs Thatcher does. It is impossible to conduct an interview with a politician of any party without the conversation coming round to her.

I have personal experience of the extent, and long range, of this domination. Some years ago I made a tour of Australia. The purpose of the trip was to puff a novel I had written, which was set in the early days of New South Wales. The publishers hawked me round from city to city, and in each place got me on to a couple of television chat shows. Sometimes there was a live studio audience, sometimes just an interviewer. These programmes were known as book-waving shows, because it was understood that, in return for five minutes of the author's time on air, he would be permitted to place a copy of his book on the coffee table between him and the interviewer, where it could be occasionally glimpsed on camera, and, at the end, pick up the book and wave it at the camera, exhibiting the title. At the same time, if you could get it in, you mentioned the name of the publisher. It was a bargain with something in it for both sides. The television station wanted a few minutes of free entertainment; the publisher wanted to sell copies of the book, and so did I.

I was allowed to wave my book. But after a day I was beginning to suspect that the book was not the real cause of the audience's interest. After two days I was certain it was not. Wherever I went, from Brisbane to Ballarat, the interviewer and his audience were really interested in Margaret Thatcher. I had seen her now and again, as any political journalist would have done, and heard her speeches, but my principal connection with Mrs Thatcher was that I had done an interview with her for the *Guardian* of London. Quite unknown to me, and without my getting a penny extra for it, this had been syndicated to newspapers across Australia. On the basis of this one hour's acquaintance, I was an authority on Mrs Thatcher.

I cannot remember how many times I told Australian audiences the story of that interview. It was always required of me. I repeated again and again how she had assured me that I would get her all wrong, and that interviews with her always came out awfully artificial. How she reasoned with my wrongheadedness, remonstrating with me and addressing me as 'My dear!' How she told me I was getting a totally false impression. How I said to her, well then, she would have little hope that what I wrote would be fair, and she replied that she would not, at which we both relaxed and laughed a bit.

I did become sick of telling this story, but it kept getting me on breakfast shows, and the book got waved, and I devised a patter which only slightly embroidered the truth. Well, I would say, we started, she and I, sitting at opposite ends of a long sofa, and I put my tape recorder, which was about the size of my book [book legitimately waved at this point], in the middle, between us. She had gone for me from the start – which was true, since she assumed that anyone from the *Guardian* must be a damp liberal of some sort, whose instruction she must undertake. And then I would describe how, as the interview progressed, so did she progress towards me, across the sofa. Until, after about an hour, I was perched right up against my end of the sofa, and the momentum of her conviction had brought her right up against me, and the only thing that separated us was my tape recorder, which was about the size of this book . . . [Here wave book.]

This account was almost true to the letter, and certainly true to the spirit, of that interview. Why the viewers of Melbourne and Sydney, at the other end of the earth, should have been so fascinated by Mrs Thatcher I never knew, but they were, and I have never forgotten this demonstration of the power of the Thatcher phenomenon. As for my book, it sold far better in Germany than in Australia.

Later on, as I talked to more members of her Cabinet, it became obvious that some, like Lord Carrington and John Nott, knew how to treat her and got on with her splendidly. They were always the ones who stood up to her. They often referred to her as Mrs T. It also became obvious that others, like Francis Pym and Michael Heseltine – two very different characters – didn't know how to deal with her and never would. From my own experience I had some small understanding why this should be.

But I was never convinced, as many politicians and journalists were and are, that she was a pitiless *laissez faire* Whig. She hadn't cut the health service to pieces. She hadn't privatized everything. She had, as Mr Simon Jenkins pointed out in the *Sunday Times* during the election, left a quarter of the electorate in council houses, and a third in some form of public employment; Britain maintained thirty per cent more civil servants than either France or West Germany, and more tax gatherers than were found necessary in the entire United States.

The American comparison is a telling one, and brings me to David Young, Lord Young, who is one of the three or four of her ministers closest to Mrs Thatcher. He made a fortune in property and banking, but by the mid-1970s, believing that liberty was vanishing under a Labour government and that Britain would end up as some kind of East Germany, he decided to emigrate to the United States. He and his wife arrived in Boston. All they heard that first night was police sirens. Next morning all they could smell was tear gas. They had arrived at the start of the bussing riots. His wife told him he must be mad. They took the first plane back home, that day.

This is a story I have from Lord Young himself, and it has never ceased to amaze me. I have felt much the same myself in New York, but I survived for two years before I came back for good. So I have reasoned that if Lord Young thinks the United States too ruthless a society, but yet is an archetypal Thatcherite, then Thatcherism cannot really be that rough, and certainly not as logically and ruthlessly *laisser faire* as its opponents would have us believe.

I also believe that Mr Kinnock's loathing of Mrs Thatcher is irrational. He cannot bring himself to utter a single good word about her. His contempt for her is so deep as to impair any hope of his gaining an understanding of her. That cannot have helped him during the election. Now by the last few days it was widely believed that he was winning if not the election then at least the campaign. But was this true? First, the campaign was not the Labour Party. That party has always been a many-faceted beast. There was a great gulf between the big Kinnock rallies and, say, the rally I have reported at Brierley Hill. That could have taken place in the seventies or the sixties. The same old hall, the same old tub-thumping: only the awful celebrity chairperson was new. And the gulf between the Kinnock campaign and the party's national headquarters in the Walworth Road, just off the Elephant and Castle, was also great. In the entrance hall hangs a portrait of Clement Attlee, presented by the old *Daily Herald* on the fiftieth anniversary of the Labour Party in 1951. On another wall hangs a framed representation of the banner of the Bethnal Green branch of the National Union of Railwaymen, circa 1900. It shows the recumbent figure of a naked man, who has apparently exhausted his strength breaking the chains which fettered him. This man is watched over by an evidently caring woman, herself most chastely dressed in flowing robes. It could be a biblical story. Then, if you walked along the corridor to the bookshop, you could ask for a copy of the Labour song sheet.

The song sheet is an old tradition. It used to cost tuppence. I remember buying one in 1974, which was after the coinage had gone decimal. It was marked 2d, and I pointed out that this meant two old pence. The party would have nothing of it. The price demanded was 2p, two new pence. This was, as I pointed out, an instant and arbitrary inflation of 240 per cent on old stock. I still had to pay. The song sheet included 'The Red Flag' – deepest red to rhyme with martyred dead, parting hymn to rhyme with gallows grim. Then there were 'The Internationale', about starvelings and servile masses; 'The Song of the AEU', about a century's darkness; and then 'The Marseillaise' and 'Uncle Tom Cobleigh and All'.

There has been some progress. The price is now 20p, an increase of 1,000 per cent in the thirteen years since 1974, and 2,400 per cent since decimalization. But 1987's song sheet has also progressed in its choice of songs. 'The Red Flag' and 'The Internationale' are still there. All the others I mentioned above have gone. There are now two Spanish revolutionary songs; one South African freedom song, in Swahili; two on equal pay for women, one about the plight of the Trico women workers; and three about disarmament – one of which is to be sung to the tune of 'The Man That Waters the Workers' Beer'. The old traditional song of that title is itself retained. The first verse goes like this:

> *Yes, I'm the man, the very fat man*
> *That waters the workers' beer.*
> *What do I care if it makes them ill,*
> *Or it makes them terribly queer?*
> *I've a car, a yacht, and an aer-o-plane,*
> *And I waters the workers' beer.*

There are also three Welsh songs, three Scottish songs, and three that are American – including 'We Shall Overcome', and one which includes the following lines:

> *'The copper bosses killed you, Joe.*
> *They shot you, Joe,' says I.*

How very English. Two other songs are sung to American tunes – 'The Red Flag' to the tune of 'Maryland', and 'Solidarity Forever' to that of 'The Battle Hymn of the Republic'. But nothing in the song sheet has much to do with a modern political party. How many gallows grim are there around today, what martyred dead, what starvelings? How many copper bosses?

But in the election there still was fear, on both sides. In the last few days both the Conservative and Labour Parties founded their newspaper advertising campaigns on nothing more subtle than fear.

Not that you would have guessed this from Mr Kinnock's last public appearance in London, on the eve of poll. He was bouncy. 'These', he said, 'are the last days of Thatcherism.' He then went on to list the characteristics of Thatcherism as arrogance and deceit, appeasement (of apartheid), sycophancy (towards America), incompetence and meanness, timidity and vanity. The vanity was that of a self-deluding empress and her courtiers.

Mr Hattersley: 'No one is dancing on our graves any more. We're a great party again.'

Mr Healey: 'You can sum up the Venice summit as the Grand Banal.'

Mrs Thatcher was then said to be suffering from neucleophilia, of which all the symptoms had been diagnosed by Dr Healey. Mr Kinnock declined an invitation to bet on the results of the election that he was going to win, and then, taking off in a great flourish of generosity, he thanked those with whom he had flown together, entrained together, laughed together, and cried together, and those who, in the last days of the campaign, had had the nobility to admit they had been wrong. I recalled no such admissions, but still it sounded fine.

But the Labour advertisements in the daily newspapers were full of doom. In Tuesday's *Guardian* the party took four full pages. On page nine a glum nurse sat with her hand to her head and with her elbow resting on a table, on which stood a kettle and two mugs. On page eleven a balding schoolteacher, with no coat or tie, stood dispiritedly in front of a blackboard with his hands on his hips. On page thirteen, an old woman sat with her hands clutching the side of her dress, in a kitchen with a clutter of cooker, cupboards, cups, saucers, a kettle, and pots, apparently of jam, all around her. On each page the reader was invited in a headline to try telling the nurse, the teacher, or the pensioner that the NHS wasn't desperately short of money, that schools weren't understaffed and under-equipped, and that pensioners had enough to live on. These were the objects of pity. On page fifteen appeared the object of loathing, Mrs Thatcher portrayed with all the photographer's art as a Cruella de Ville, with the light in the wrong place everywhere: under her picture appeared an invitation to try telling her she was wrong.

Well, she may have been. But as for the other three pages, seldom can so much money have been spent pointlessly portraying misery. Of course there are pensioners who are poor, but as for the other two, the urge was to advise the nurse not to show so obviously that she was tired, and perhaps to tidy up the clutter around her; and, as for the teacher, you recognized with a sinking heart that there were only too many of the dreary likes of him, and wanted to tell him, at the least, to get properly dressed. Who would want such a man to teach his children?

The heart sank. But political ads succeed best when they lift the heart, or at least the expectations – when they show what is better, and what can be done. The Salvation Army knows this. When it shows a destitute old woman, or a wretched child, it also shows that woman or child being encouraged, helped, or in some way lifted up, by a figure in the uniform of the Salvation Army. There are no political prizes for the simple portrayal of misery. It is just a costly waste of money.

The Conservatives, that last morning of the campaign, were not making a great show of jumping up and down. Mrs Thatcher was saying plainly that the Labour Party was now totally different from the party of Attlee, of Gaitskell, and even of Wilson or Callaghan. People now feared it as they had not done before. Their fear was enhanced because they knew the Militants had been kept quiet, because Labour knew the way the Militants did things would strike fear into people's hearts. She didn't know whether the Conservatives had got this over well enough. Then she said: 'There were times during the past eight years when, believing passionately as I do in the things we were doing, I began to wonder whether there was still the enterprise in Britain that had made her the country she was, or whether, having got the ball to people's feet, they would still have that vivacity, verve, the energy, the vigour, the dynamism, that the merchant venturers used to have. I know now that they have. It has worked . . . It is what it is all about. It is what I believe is the British character. How did we get on to all this?'

It was an expression of honest doubt, doubt since overcome but nevertheless doubt: it had the ring of truth.

Then Lord Whitelaw, who had said practically nothing for weeks, did say something. 'I do not know when we went into an election with a better case to put before the people, and I do not know of an election where I had more fear of what might happen if we found the Labour Party wrecking the whole thing, which I believe they would if anyone was unwise enough to vote for them tomorrow. If I have not said anything else in this election, that is rather a good thing to start with.'

Did Mrs Thatcher agree that while Mr Kinnock appealed to the voters' hearts, and Dr Owen to their minds, she appealed to their wallets?

Plainly her only answer to that was no, but she ended this way: 'The most important motivating factor in human life is the desire by your own efforts to do better for your own children. This is in tune with the deepest instincts of the British people. To me, it is in tune with the deepest morality.'

On Tuesday, Wednesday, and Thursday of that last week the Conservatives were taking three whole pages a day in each of the newspapers that mattered to them – *The Times*, *Telegraph*, *Guardian*, *Mail*, *Express*, and so on. The whole burden of the message was that things had got better under Mrs Thatcher. It was Mrs Thatcher's turn this time to be saying 'You've never had it so good', with the added warning that Labour would spoil everything. In 1959, the Conservatives' message, under Macmillan, was 'Don't Let Labour Ruin It'. Mrs Thatcher came very close to saying that. The simplest message, and the most telling, was the following, which was spelled out in large type across a whole page: 'BRITAIN IS GREAT AGAIN. DON'T LET LABOUR WRECK IT. VOTE CONSERVATIVE.'

Then there were the advertisements not paid for by Central Office but by the Committee for a Free Britain, and distinctly in the Conservative interest. A typical one said, and again all this was just large type and lots of white space on a full page: 'My name is Betty Sheridan. I live in Haringey. I'm married with two children. And I'm scared. If you vote Labour they'll go on teaching my kids about GAYS & LESBIANS instead of giving them proper lessons.'

The advertising managers of the national newspapers were delighted, and were the first to credit the assertion that days of greatness were upon them.

Whether the Labour campaign had won the election or not remained to be seen, although the polls were still putting the Conservatives eight points ahead, as they had throughout the campaign. But what was already certain was that the Labour campaign had established Mr Kinnock. Since the first week he had been and remained the undoubted leader, even though Bryan Gould, who took most of his morning press conferences, was obviously the brighter of the two men, and had a firmer grasp of his party's policies. And it

was true that the imperial image of Mr Kinnock had been
deliberately moderated a little. The *Ecce Homo* election commercial had been broadcast a second time, it was said by Mr
Kinnock's own decision, but it had been slightly and tactfully
adapted. At the start, a woman's voice read out these words:
'A great many of you have asked us to show the following
election broadcast. [No mention that it was a second showing.] It presents the views and values of the Labour Party
through its leader, Neil Kinnock.' And at the end, instead
of just the name Kinnock, the word Labour appeared on the
screen, with the red rose, and the statement that the country
was crying out for change.

But still, given that the campaign had worked for Kinnock, had it worked for Labour? Sir Paul Bryan, the retiring
member for Boothferry, who had been Minister of State for
Employment in the Heath government, found, as he went
round the Yorkshire constituencies, that the campaign
worked well enough to convince waverers that Labour
might win – whereupon they were promptly converted to
Conservatism.

The poll was still a day away. Had Labour's campaign
succeeded gloriously? Or had it backfired? Had those who
might have voted for the Alliance, had the Don't Knows,
been convinced by it into voting Conservative? Had Labour
put the fear of Labour into them? It remained to be seen.

FIFTEEN

Hogarth's 'Third Administration'

Mrs Thatcher looked to be on the verge of winning her third successive election, and you had to go back as far as Robert Banks Jenkinson, second Earl of Liverpool, to find anyone else who had done that. Liverpool has a reputation in schoolboy history as a villain, for his ruthlessness in putting down the rebellious lower orders of his day. That is about all that is remembered, and undoubtedly, if he had been confronted with Arthur Scargill, his whole instinct would have been to act once again as he did in the bad years from 1817-19. Mr Scargill would have found *Habeas Corpus* suspended, seditious meetings prohibited, and picketing outside Orgreave coke works put down by the militia.

But Liverpool had his good points. He insisted on the prohibition of the slave trade. And all in all his instincts were sound. At the age of nineteen, having just left Oxford, and happening to be in Paris, he witnessed the fall of the Bastille. Before he came of age, and while he was still a commoner, he was elected to Parliament for the rotten borough of Appleby, but still spent much of his time travelling round a Europe which was in revolution, of which he disapproved. In 1793, being properly outraged at the murder by guillotine of Louis XVI, he wanted to declare war on France immediately. He was too young to see this was done. It would later have saved him the trouble of defeating Napoleon, a little matter which was achieved under his administration, after he became Prime Minister in 1812. He is not remembered as a wartime Prime Minister, only for putting down riots, but he did beat Napoleon. Perhaps Liverpool lacked conspicuous magnanimity, but he was a realist. After Waterloo it was he who decided to exile Napoleon to St Helena, though he privately wrote to Castlereagh, another villain of schoolboy history, that he wished the restored King of France would shoot the man and be done with it. This was, of course, something an English gentleman could not do himself. Liverpool's private life was irreproachable.

But at the end of the election campaign I was thinking a bit further back than Liverpool, to Hogarth, and reflecting how he would have loved the last few days of it all. So I shall essay three sketches of these last days of an English election – 'Election Engravings', as it were, after Hogarth's prints of that name, done about 1755.

The Election Entertainment

I take not the degrading Wembley showbiz rally, but the last of the Prime Minister's series of election press conferences which were attended daily by the hacks of the world. A. J. Liebling of the *New Yorker* maintained that there were three kinds of journalists. They were the reporter, who writes what he sees; the interpretative reporter, who writes what he sees and what he construes to be its meaning; and the expert, who writes what he construes to be the meaning of what he hasn't seen. All three kinds were represented daily at Smith Square. There were always plenty of experts, some of whom rarely left their offices at all, and certainly never travelled on an election campaign, but who felt able to take a taxi as far as Smith Square, and then wrote copiously. Now sagacious questions were asked by the likes of these, and by other celebrated columnists – about great gulfs and deep divisions, trade balances and law and order, and so on. The revealing pieces of trivia, the asides, were seldom reported, but I shall have a go.

What lessons [a dangerous question, this, from the very

good reporter of the *Financial Times*] did Mrs Thatcher feel she had learned over the last four weeks?

Prime Minister: 'Had I not been as open to questions as I have been, you might have crucified me. As it is, some of you might have a go.'

How [this question put by a disembodied voice over a loudspeaker from an overflow meeting] did she justify her policies to the millions who lived in misery, when she was probably wealthier than she ever had been in her life?

Prime Minister: 'What a strange question. With all due respect, I think that would apply to most Prime Ministers. I do not know whether you are suggesting that we have a system of anarchy, but I would be against that.'

She had [this from an obvious sceptic] just described sympathetically her own good fortune in having a London seat and a wealthy husband which enabled her to pursue her career . . .

Prime Minister: 'I do not think that I said that.'

But she had implied it?

Prime Minister: 'No, I am sorry – look . . .'

The questioner begged her pardon: her husband had had a job in London, then. Did she regard her own good fortune as luck or judgment?

Prime Minister: 'Most people need a little bit of luck in life. I do sometimes say to young candidates who are trying to get a seat that the first seat I fought was in 1950; the first time I got into Parliament was in 1959. It is known as resolution, persistence, perseverance, consistency, *et cetera*.'

Questioner: Though she looked as beautiful as she had eight years before, did she have someone in mind – he was not asking for a name – whom she was nursing to come after her in twenty years' time?

Mr Tebbit, answering this one for the Prime Minister: 'It has to be somebody who is just as good-looking?'

Then there was Mr Edwin Roth who was everlastingly asking earnest questions in a thick German accent on behalf of miscellaneous German language newspapers which he prefers not to name, for fear that they should be jealous of each other. He says he does not have a thick German accent, just a thick Schoenbrunnian accent, which he says every German would know as the accent of the cultured Viennese. He also says, at length, that he has been at it since he was eighteen, and has cross-examined François Mitterand, Ronald Reagan, and even Nikita Krushchev. That last morning of the election he had already been told by Neil Kinnock that if a way could be found of disinventing nuclear weapons he would certainly invite Mr Roth for experimentation. But Mr Roth is not a man to be put down so easily as that, and I certify that what follows is a verbatim transcript of his last question, an hour or so later, to Mrs Thatcher.

Roth of Schoenbrunn: 'Prime Minister, I attended the last ever coronation of a Pope [merry laughter], which was an absolutely magnificent ceremony. Even without lasers, it was fantastic. [Loud laughter.] It will never happen again. The most impressive moment at that ceremony was when a black-dressed monk [howls of laughter], very simply dressed [more howls], three times approached the Pope, burned some flax, and shouted out, "*Sic transit gloria mundi.*" [Helpless laughter.] Do you think that when a Prime Minister wins three successive elections, one might set a precedent for a similar adaptation of that in the House of Commons?' [People fall about.]

Prime Minister: 'I am sure that you will suffer withdrawal symptoms when we no longer have press conferences every morning, Mr Roth.'

John Moore, Transport Secretary and an up-and-coming favourite, sitting on the platform with Mrs Thatcher that morning: 'Prime Minister, I will do so much for you in our country, but wearing a dress and muttering odd imprecations in Latin is, I'm afraid, one of the very few things I would resist.' [More yelps.]

Here Mr Tebbit, to restore gravity, announces that drinks will be served later.

The Polling

Hendon Town Hall. Thursday evening. The count of Mrs Thatcher's Finchley vote.

10.30 p.m. Outside, hordes of police. Inside, a mob – packed into what looks like the smallest town hall in England and already baking under television lights two hours before anything is due to happen.

You get in past the tightest security of the campaign. For the first and only time a metal detector detects something on me – first the coins in my pocket, then my keys, then the chains which fasten my two passes round my neck.

10.45 p.m. Upstairs, the apparently innocent photographer of the *Star* is thrown out by the police. Fellow photographers mutter about the heavies of the Met. The portrait of Councillor Brook Flowers, JP, Mayor of Hendon in the jubilee year of 1934-35, looks down as a second photographer, half drunk, tries to pick a fight with a policewoman, and to rally his colleagues to protest. 'Suppose', he says, 'we go f--- home and leave the f--- Prime Minister to it?' No one leaves.

There are two fringe candidates, each as much entitled as Mrs Thatcher to a place in the hall and a seat on the platform. The Gremloid candidate espouses a defence policy of intergalactic starfighters, promises free BMX bikes to everyone under eighteen, and proposes to create Hartlepool the capital of Britain.

11.15 p.m. The Gremloid candidate is at first refused admission because his head and face are covered by a huge black hat, and hats are not permitted in the council chamber. He explains that he is Lord Buckethead, and that the hat is not a hat but an essential part of his person containing his brains. He is allowed to remain.

12.40 a.m. A noisy young woman in a tutu, the official Gold candidate, enters the chamber. Her policies are 24-carat-gold rings and a million pounds for every voter. She looks at the seats allotted to candidates, and sees that only Mrs Thatcher has been provided with mineral water.

'She's only a candidate too. No mineral water for me, none for her. I'll remove it.'

She seizes Mrs Thatcher's two bottles of Ashbourne water – 'nothing but the sparkle added to the fresh water that has filtered down through the hills' – and does remove them from the chamber, stalked by a police superintendent who is in two minds what to do about her. He does nothing. She then returns calling in a loud voice, 'Just because she may be Prime Minister!'

12.55 a.m. Enter an official with one bottle of Ashbourne for each candidate. Cheers from the rabble of hacks trampling over each other in the gallery, fighting to stand on seats, on the arms of seats, and on portable step ladders imported for the occasion. The integrity of the Press is questioned from the body of the hall. The hacks and the friends of the candidates then bait each other on and off for half an hour.

1.31 a.m. The returning officer announces that the said Margaret Hilda Thatcher is duly . . . [Boos, cheers, jeers, gavel thumping.] Margaret Hilda Thatcher starts to make her acceptance speech, is howled down, stops, quells the rabble with a killing look, and offers general thanks, and so on. Outside, there are enough police to control the Cup Final.

Chairing the Member

The return of the victorious Prime Minister to Conservative Central Office, Smith Square.

This is Hogarth country. The tremendous church of St John, in the centre of the square, built by Thomas Archer about 1725, was new when Hogarth did his engravings of 'The Rake's Progress', and still young when he did his 'Election Prints'. The houses around, in Lord North Street, are of the same date. From such houses, and from such sash windows, Hogarthian molls could have leaned and not looked out of place.

Outside, the carousing generality stands shoulder to shoulder in the square and sprawls over the steps leading up to the portico of St John's; all is brilliantly lit by television lights.

Inside, a smaller mob, just arrived from the scrimmage at Finchley, falls on the opera-supper laid out there – pâté, vol-au-vents, chicken drumsticks, and wine shipped in by Jean Voisier et Cie.

2.34 a.m. Mrs Thatcher, shown on close circuit riding back from Finchley in her armour-plated Daimler, already has her majority. It has all been settled for some time. Mr Kinnock on television says the country has voted for division. The SDP puts on a good show of surprise as it falls everywhere to bits.

3.00 a.m. Outside, the crowd raggedly sings 'Jerusalem'. Inside, it is calculated that Mrs Thatcher needs to remain Prime Minister until the following January to beat Asquith's twentieth-century record of eight years and eight months without a break.

3.09 a.m. Mrs Thatcher arrives. Mr Tebbit gives her red roses, repossessed from the Labour Party. Then she makes her staircase speech. 'This is a day of history,' she says. [Yelps and hurrahs.] This great country. The greater the trust the greater the duty. These islands. No slacking. Parties tonight, clear up tomorrow, but on Monday big job to do – inner cities. [This is a new tack, so new that it is instantly noticed even after four weeks of continuous performance and several glasses of Jean Voisier's red.] Get right back in there. Absolutely marvellous.

A photographer recording this great moment is plucked just in time from a collapsing heap of four chairs on which he is perched to get a better shot.

3.10 a.m. Bedlam.

3.20 a.m. Cecil Parkinson arrives with wife. An end to speculation there. Whoever's in, whoever's out, he's in.

3.30 a.m. The platform from which Mrs Thatcher launched her manifesto in chaos three and a half weeks before is now tidily littered with half-gnawed and discarded chicken bones, and glasses containing only dregs.

3.57 a.m. Lord Young arrives. Gels drift down into the

hall from the private party upstairs calling out, 'Hiya'. Mrs Thatcher's reappearance on the staircase is imminently expected. A woman leaning against a wall calls out, 'Come on, Mags.'

4.00 a.m. First Central Office gel takes instinctive initiative and propositions Conservative man. He does not immediately comprehend. She is amused. He comprehends. An assignation is fixed for the weekend. She kisses his ear. It is like something out of Bergman's *Hamlet* which has just been on at the National. The Court of Denmark at play.

4.01 a.m. Second Central Office gel, languidly composed and holding a dish of strawberries and cream, leans against the lift door and asks a man holding a two-thirds empty bottle of champagne, 'Tell me, who are you? Oh. Is Mr X [naming a famous television commentator] married?'

4.06 a.m. Mark Thatcher and his American wife come downstairs and are much photographed. Cameraman: 'Would you do it on the stairs please?' Mr Thatcher, jun., leads his bride back up a few steps and both smile as in a network soap.

4.12 a.m. 'More flags!' exclaims a gel. More flags are brought down and taken out to be waved in the square.

4.15 a.m. Mrs Thatcher descends the staircase. 'High time', she admonishes everyone, 'that you went to bed.'

Brave hack: 'Denis, how do you feel about it?'

Mr Denis Thatcher, defiantly: 'Fine.'

Mrs Thatcher: 'No more parties tonight.' She appears to be about to continue.

4.17 a.m. Mr Denis Thatcher, firmly: 'Good night, gentlemen.'

Outside it is already light, and the third administration dawns.

Afterword

This is a brief word about what happened to some of the people in this book, the characters of the story.

Mrs Thatcher won with a majority of one hundred seats. Only four out of fifty-nine political journalists asked by the *Spectator* before the election predicted a majority of that size – which only goes to show how fallible the Fourth Estate is – though forty-nine did predict an overall Conservative majority.

To almost universal surprise, Mr Tebbit, of his own free will, retired from the Cabinet. To no one's surprise Mr Biffen was sacked. Thereupon he astonished almost everyone who knew him by describing Mrs Thatcher's regime, in which he had after all served for seven years, as Stalinist. He later said this was a colourful phrase and not a personal attack. Mr Parkinson returned to the Cabinet. Mr Moore, the man who said he would do anything for Mrs Thatcher except put on a dress, was promoted. The Conservative candidates won at both Hornchurch and Chelmsford. There was no avalanche in the West Country.

On the Labour side, Mr Kinnock collected much credit for the style of the campaign which had not won the election. Mr Healey, after twenty-three years on the front bench, retired from the Shadow Cabinet, which lost much tone thereby. Mr Smith, he who addressed the Brierley Hill rally, became Shadow Chancellor. Many of the rest bickered among themselves. Mr Hattersley, who had a dim campaign, attacked Mr Gould's proposals for a new image, saying the party could not be sold to voters with the language of soap powders and dog food: they should stick to the Sermon on the Mount. In return, Mr Gould defended the glitz and glitter of his campaign and suggested there might be a generation gap between himself and Mr Hattersley. Within a week of the election, five Labour whips resigned or were sacked. Mr Livingstone, having reduced the Labour majority by two-thirds in what used to be the safe seat of Brent East, made a maiden speech giving comfort to the IRA. Miss Abbott did better than expected in Hackney, almost maintained the 1983 majority there, and became the first black woman MP. Ms Deirdre Wood failed again to take Greenwich, leaving Rosie Barnes, a political innocent, as one of the few remaining members of a party which had by then lost its innocence. Mrs Betty Boothroyd, the former Tiller girl, was named as a deputy speaker of the Commons. Glenys Kinnock was a big success for Labour throughout the campaign. Out electioneering one day she firmly declined to *pretend* to play with some children for the benefit of the cameras. When the cameras left, she knelt down and talked to the children. This was noticed and admired even by Fleet Street's finest, who thought the world of her for it.

The Alliance fell to bits, winning only twenty-two seats in all. The SDP won only five. The Sunday after the election Mr Steel put himself forward as candidate for the leadership of a new and united party to be called the Liberal-Democratic Alliance, saying that the existing half-way house was doomed. This was only what the late and lamented David Penhaligon had been saying for years. Merge or else, he would say, having first made everyone roll with laughter at the spectre of a party with two heads. And do it now, he would say: because, you know, time was a great eroder of goodwill. So now, too late, after another squandered election, Mr Steel was calling for a merger. Otherwise, he said, it would be better for the Liberals and the SDP to go their separate ways rather than be 'locked forever in a wary and weary partnership of which the only guiding constitutional principle was mutual suspicion'. It was a bit quick, but otherwise can have surprised only those who did not recognize the obvious – that Mr Steel is a strong and ambitious man. The idea of him as a puppet in Dr Owen's pocket was always nonsense. Of the original SDP Gang of Four, Mr Rogers, Mr Jenkins, and Mrs Williams – none of whom by then had a seat – supported this proposal for a merger. Dr Owen stood out against it. He said it was defeatist, listed the issues on which the two parties had chronically disagreed – something that could now presumably be admitted – and tossed in the aside that it was always liberals with a small 'l' whose nerves failed. He would not join a merged party. If necessary, he would sit in Parliament on his own. The two Davids had still been stating at their last rally – though no doubt with cordial wariness and weariness – that they had found the right degreee of togetherness and apartness, but now they had come apart. The Alliance was stone dead, the SDP had both feet in the grave, and it looked as though Dr Owen could only extend the line of distinguished politicians who had found themselves without a real party – Oswald Mosley and Enoch Powell being the most obvious examples.

It would be reasonable for anyone to ask why so many political reporters didn't foresee all this and say so. They did foresee it, but their first business was to report the game that was still in progress. Like many others, I never gave the Alliance a dog's chance after 1983. There were always too many ifs and buts. In 1987 the whole edifice had to be constructed on the rickety hope of a hung Parliament, which was never really on. And the two Alliance parties had taken five years to agree on so elementary and necessary a thing as a single party colour. They fought the 1983 election with at least three. Dr Owen, Mr Steel, Mr Jenkins – all three of them – thought the matter trivial and said so. If they really thought that, they were never going to win much, not in an era when elections are nationally televized, and television is in colour. If on the other hand they just couldn't agree on a colour, what sort of omen was that? Then there was the name SDP itself. British political parties don't have initials for their name. For a couple of years after the SDP's foundation it was common to hear members call their own party the SPD, which were the more familiar initials of the German social democrats. As late as 1987 there was confusion about names, which the Alliance leaders pig-headedly refused to acknowledge. Last June I asked one woman if she was going to vote Alliance, she said no; she was for the SDP. One of the shrewdest political comments I saw during the election was scrawled on an Alliance poster in the Farringdon Road, London. It was the poster that showed the two Davids and called them 'The Only Fresh Thing on the Menu'. Someone had added these words, 'Sell-by date June 11'.

But why didn't people whose business was politics know that Owen and Steel were miles apart? The answer again is that everybody did. It was obvious. That morning in the pub on the edge of Dartmoor, when Dr Owen was asked if the Tweedledum and Tweedledee thing had sorted itself out, what was his reply? 'Helped by fog.' It was fog which had delayed Mr Steel's arrival in Plymouth the night before. The tone of this reply was nothing new. When Owen and Steel met at Plymouth in the previous election, what invitation did Mr Owen make when he saw Mr Steel's despised battlebus approaching? He said: 'Want to come and see the great political love-in?' And when he and David Steel met, they went and sat in the middle of a large lawn to get away from cameras and reporters. It seemed an amiable chat. There were fond speculations. David Owen later said, after the election was over, that what Mr Steel proposed that afternoon was the deposition in mid-election of Roy Jenkins, who was then Alliance Prime Minister-designate. David Owen didn't forget that. He must have told everybody. The straight answer is that everybody knew how the two Davids didn't get on, but it was an old story. It just wasn't worth repeating over and over again. Which was hard luck on those previously apolitical men and women who joined the SDP thinking it wasn't just another political party. If you believed that, it must be all the more disillusion-ing to see Dr Owen and Mrs Williams going for each other with knives.

The present importance of the Alliance is only as an example of hope betrayed. It does not much matter what it calls itself in future, if it has a future. At the end of a book of reportage I have one suggestion to make, and that is to the Labour Party. It changed its campaign. Whatever Mr Kinnock's protestations to the contrary, it has practically abandoned the colour red. It will change its policies. But Labour – though in 1901 and 1945 a good word, and a word with meaning – is now a word with no visible attraction. Not all that many people now work with their hands, and even if they all voted together it would not be enough to elect a majority party. Besides, Labour now sounds the party of losers. Along with everything else, the party might try changing its name.

So much for the parties and politicians. The certainties of Mrs Thatcher have prevailed. The certainties of Sheffield and Silverwood will not have been dissipated by a Conservative parliamentary majority of one hundred. Their certainties will still be there. I do not think that young face worker was right when he said that if *She* won, Broadwater Farm was going to look like a picnic, up north anyway. I hope he was not right. I hope also that the extraordinary energies of Mrs Thatcher – intolerant though they are, and at times intolerable – may be turned, in part, to the huge task of making something of the lives of those people. This is now a poor country. Her toughness is more likely to help than all Mr Kinnock's caring.

So I shall end by recalling two moments. The first came at the end, and is of Mrs Thatcher in the moment of her victory, on the staircase, amid the champagne and strawberr-ies.

'We have a great deal to do. No one must slack. Parties tonight, clean up tomorrow, but on Monday, you know, we've got a big job to do in some of those inner cities.' As usual, she meant it.

The second moment came at the beginning of the campaign, at Silverwood late at night, as I was about to leave the club which had been a soup kitchen in the miners' strike. It is of Mrs Gwen Mellors, the nurse, saying: 'When she first came in, I thought it might do the country some good. A woman. To bring up a family. But she's never had to want. To be honest, say she gets elected again, and she puts my sons in employment, then I tell you what, the next time she came up I'd vote for her. But she won't.'

Well?

July 1987

Index